From Abram To Abraham

Study Guide

Flying Eagle Publications

Unless otherwise noted, all Scripture King James Version of the Bible. Public Domain.

Scripture quotations marked (BBE) are taken from the 1949/1964 BIBLE IN BASIC ENGLISH, public domain.

"Scripture taken from the Literal Translation of the Holy Bible Copyright © 1976 - 2000
By Jay P. Green, Sr.
Used by permission of the copyright holder."

All word meanings from *Strong's Exhaustive Concordance,* Strong, James. 1890. *Strong's Exhaustive Concordance of the Bible.* Abingdon Press.

From Abram To Abraham
ISBN:978-1-7327688-7-1
Flying Eagle Publications.com

Cover Image: Eddie and Carolina Stigson courtesy of Unsplash.
Illustration: Haley Jula.

©2022 Flying Eagle Publications LLC. All Rights Reserved under International Copyright Law. No part of this book may be reproduced or transmitted in any form by any means.

Printed in the United States.

Table of Contents

Teacher Guide..7
Assignment Schedule...9
Small Group Leader Lesson Planner Template................13
Chapter 1 Devotion..15
General Questions...21
Chapter 1 Evaluation/Test..27
Chapter 2 Devotion..29
General Questions...33
 Chapter 2 Evaluation/Test...39
Chapter 3 Devotion..41
General Questions...45
Chapter 3 Evaluation/Test..49
Chapter 4 Devotion..51
General Questions...55
Chapter 4 Evaluation/Test..59
Chapter 5 Devotion..61
General Questions...65
Chapter 5 Evaluation/Test..69
Chapter 6 Devotion..71

General Questions..75
Chapter 6 Evaluation/Test..79
Chapter 7 Devotion...81
General Questions..85
Chapter 7 Evaluation/Test..89
Chapter 8 Devotion...91
General Questions..95
Chapter 8 Evaluation/Test..99
Chapter 9 Devotion...101
General Questions..105
Chapter 9 Evaluation/Test..107
Answer Keys..109

Introduction to Study Guide

We like choices. In this guide we've given you the ability to adapt it to your purpose. Do you need discussion questions for a youth or small group study or a more formalized way of assessing learning because you are a homeschool or private school educator? Perhaps you are interested in pursuing your own spiritual growth? Will you need ideas for further study?

We've got you covered.

While any of the questions may be used to enhance discussions of the reading material, some are geared toward academic learning for the purpose of apologetics. Tests are provided if you need them. Answers to most questions are at the back of the book. Obviously some questions are meant for personal reflection and the answers to these will vary.

The Drawing Near Sections are application activities for devotional time. They are located after the longer devotions at the beginning of each chapter and at the end of the General Questions section for each chapter. Use either of these for your personal devotion time or for your students.

The For Further Study and Activity sections are optional. One or two could be chosen and assigned as part of the overall course or as weekly group projects for small groups, co-ops or classrooms. A lesson plan for homeschooling is provided as an example for a nine week course with tests to evaluate learning. This plan could be adapted for the classroom.

Of course no adult in a small group or otherwise wants to have to do formal projects and tests, so ignore all the heavy duty school lingo. Gather the discussion material you want to use for each session, use an activity to break up the weekly routine if you wish, and choose an application so people can interact with Jesus. We've provided a lesson template for you to organize your thoughts. Happy learning!

Abraham

Leader Guide

We've created two pathways to use this guide in an academic or homeschool setting. They are listed below. A daily assignment schedule follows. We recommend Guided Learning for the best results. You can, however, adapt and blend either method to create an individualized experience.

Guided Learning: *Pre-assign reading of full chapter on student's time. Do not follow reading schedule.* This method allows for the student to read the chapter as a whole. After they've completed the chapter, discuss portions of the chapter each day as the Assignment Schedule instructs to reinforce learning. Student may read the Devotion from the Study Guide on first day of each chapter discussion. Use the daily schedule to review information contained in the chapter and to discuss assigned questions. Talk about any points, facts or discoveries you or the student(s) think are important for that portion. Assign an Activity or Further Study as a project for the week. This may be a group project if desired. Use the Chapter Evaluation to record or assess learning. Test may be used as a quiz on Day 4 and corrected. Reteach any problem areas. Take test again on Day 5.

- Teacher Responsibility: Be familiar with material. Make sure chapter gets read before daily discussion schedule starts. Guide daily discussions 20-30 minutes. Assign any Activities or Further Studies for week and discuss or check. Reteach any problem areas. Conduct whichever testing procedure you prefer. *Bonus Teacher Tip:* Use answer key section when asking students questions because the answer is right in front of you– just in case you forgot the material. This saves time and boy, do you look smart!

- Student Responsibility: Read book and Devotion from Study Guide. Take notes of any information desired. Partake in discussion. Give presentation of completed Activity or Further Study. Keep a folder for all material. Complete review and evaluation for chapter.

Independent Student Learning: Have student keep a notebook to answer the assigned questions. Use the daily schedule to assign reading and questions. Check each day's questions. Choose Activity or Further Study to be completed for each chapter. These are optional, if pressed for time. They may also be completed on student's own time and shared or collected when you choose. Student should take test after chapter work is completed.

- Teacher's Responsibility: Prepare for successful learning. Photocopy assignment schedule, questions and test for student if they are not using the Study Guide. Check answers to daily questions so student is reviewing correct information. Assign Activity or Further Study for the week and check. Check test answers.

- Student's Responsibility: Keep a folder of all material. Complete daily readings, assigned questions, activity projects and review. Review and take test after each chapter.

Assignment Schedule

- Read pages listed to quotation that marks the last paragraph to be read for the day. Continue from next paragraph on following day. On Day 4 you will finish reading the chapter.
- Complete questions assigned for each day after reading selection.
- Guided Learning students should read Devotion from Study Guide on Day 1 for each chapter and be ready to discuss questions assigned for the page content covered for Days 1-4 for each chapter.

Chapter 1 Of Names and Family

Day 1: Read Devotion (GL). Read pgs 7-11 to "...there might be later." Answer questions 1-3.
Day 2: Read pgs 11-16 to "...a royal official." Answer question 4.
Day 3: Read pgs 16-21 to "...Old Testament judges." Answer questions 5-7.
Day 4: Read pgs 21-25. Answer questions 8-10.
Day 5: Review and take test.

Chapter 2 Called Out From Ur

Day 1: Read Devotion (GL). Read pgs 27-31 "...pick your favorite Ur."
Day 2: Read pgs 31-37 to "But does the Bible?" Answer questions 1-3.
Day 3: Read pgs 37-41 to "...'Leave this behind you.' " Answer ques-

tions 4-7.
Day 4: Read pgs 41-46. Answer questions 8-15.
Day 5: Review and take test.

Chapter 3 Canaan

Day 1: Read Devotion (GL). Read pgs 49-54 to "...may have looked good to Terah." Answer questions 1-5.
Day 2: Read pgs 54-59 to "...north, south, east and west." Answer questions 6-7.
Day 3: Read pgs 59-65 to "...were made in Turkey." Answer questions 8-17.
Day 4: Read pgs 65-71. Answer questions 18-24.
Day 5: Review and take test.

Chapter 4 The Egypt Incident

Day 1: Read Devotion (GL). Read pgs 73-78 to "...time of Abraham and even before." Answer questions 1-4.
Day 2: Read pgs 78-84 to "He needed God." Answer questions 5-7.
Day 3: Read pgs 84-90 to "...built his future from them." Answer questions 8-11.
Day 4: Read pgs 90-93. Answer questions 12-15.
Day 5: Review and take test.

Chapter 5 The Not So Legendary Battle of Siddim

Day 1: Read Devotion (GL). Read pgs 95-100 to "...Genesis 14 a myth." Answer questions 1-4.

Day 2: Read pgs 100-105 to "...for Eri-Aku." Answer questions 5-6.
Day 3: Read pgs 105-111 to "...Negev sites were a match." Answer questions 7-10.
Day 4: Read pgs 111- 118. Answer questions 11-20
Day 5: Review and take test.

Chapter 6 Making Abraham

Day 1: Read Devotion (GL). Read pgs 119-126 to "...answered Abraham's complaint and fears." Answer questions 1-10.
Day 2: Read pgs 126-134 to "So Hagar ran away." Answer questions 11-17.
Day 3: Read pgs 134-141 to "...against later archaeological finds." Answer questions 18-22.
Day 4: Read pgs 141-148. Answer questions 23-25.
Day 5: Review and take test.

Chapter 7 Sodom and Ishmael:Paying the Piper

Day 1: Read Devotion (GL). Read pgs 149-154 to "...the cave today near Safi." Answer questions 1-7.
Day 2: Read pgs 154-160 to "...make them leave Sodom." Answer questions 8-14.
Day 3: Read pgs 160-165 to "...had to take care of." Answer questions 15-16.
Day 4: Read pgs 165-170. Answer questions 17-24.
Day 5: Review and take test.

Chapter 8 The Binding of Isaac

Day 1: Read Devotion (GL). Read pgs 171-176 to "...consequences are up to us." Answer questions 1-6.

Day 2: Read pgs 176-182 to "...so we remember who really owns it." Answer questions 7-18.

Day 3: Read pgs 182-188 to "...was about protecting Abraham's lineage." Answer questions 19-22.

Day 4: Read pgs 189-194. Answer questions 23-25.

Day 5: Review and take test.

Chapter 9 Abraham's Legacy

Day 1: Read Devotion (GL). Read pgs 195-199 to "...day we know nothing about." Answer questions 1-4.

Day 2: Read pgs 199-204 to "...Romans 4:18-22." Answer questions 5-10.

Day 3: Read pgs 204- 208. Answer questions 11-14.

Day 4: Read "If you have never asked Jesus into your heart, start here."

Day 5: Review and take test. Time to celebrate! You are done!

Group Leader Template

To Do: Read chapter from book and Devotion from Study Guide. Pray for students and for wisdom.

To List: Chapter and Devotion high points, facts, discoveries I thought important and note the page number of each. These are my talking points, but I will ask my students what they learned from the chapter too and include their input throughout the lesson.

To Choose: The verses I am focusing on and will teach from.

To Decide: What I want the class to know and remember. This is my teaching focus. What Drawing Near application will I use?

To Pick: Questions I want to cover and discuss. (Tip: Have the Guide with you in case you have time to ask more than you have chosen.)

To Pick: At least one activity to do during discussion time to provide variety to class flow. I can break up class into groups for this. (Tip: Always plan more than you think you will need in case you have to fill time.)

To Remember: Some students will not have read the portion for the week or I may have new students, so I am ready to explain, explain and patiently explain.
My Notes:

Chapter 1

Of Names and Family

Devotion

Have your Bible, a journal and pen handy. Look up the verses quoted. Read them, the verses around them, and write down what you learn.

Abraham began life as Abram, son of an idol worshipper, citizen of Aram of the two rivers and husband to a barren wife. This was his identity. Not the expected image of an exalted father is it? But Abraham's inner identity became something else.

Included in a proverb about a selfish man is a basic truth that states, "As a man thinks in his heart so is he." (Proverbs 23:7) It reminds us our inner thoughts and beliefs are a more accurate picture of ourselves. Another proverb informs us that out of the heart flow the issues, *tôtsâ'âh*, or boundaries (source or place from which anything goes forth) of life. (Proverbs 4:23)

We are told to protect our heart because the issues of life flow from it, and we guard it by hearing God's word, keeping it in front of our eyes and in the middle of our heart. "Let them not depart from thine eyes; keep them in the midst of thine heart. For they are life unto those that find them, and health to all their flesh." (Proverbs 4:20-21.)

The word translated health is *marpê'* which means a curative or a medicine. But notice God's words are "found," *mâtsâ'*, to attain or acquire. These are words you choose to possess.

What we believe to be true we act on and we speak. This is why the process forms our identity because it determines what we think possible and establishes our destiny. This is also why it is important to know what God has said about who we are in Him, and it is even more important to believe what He says to the point of being fully persuaded because that is the place of faith. Knowing what God has said is not faith. Admiring what He said is not faith. Receiving into your heart and acting on, or because of, His word is faith.

The Bible says not everyone has the faith of God. And yet, everyone operates on faith. Are you surprised? Not if you realize faith is trust or confidence. Romans 10:17 shows us another principle. Trust and confidence come to us through hearing. It works by listening with our mind's ear. A person can hear the words of their friend, professor, instructor, doctor, nurse, mechanic, banker or accountant and become fully persuaded. When a person puts their confidence and trust in what is said and acts on it, they've moved from knowledge to faith in that advice and taken it as their authority.

Faith exists at a deeper level than knowledge, and it requires a corresponding action. For example, if you believe the pond is frozen enough to skate on, you will skate on it. It is the world's adage of putting your money where your mouth is. We are constantly choosing what we believe and trust and making decisions based on those choices.

Our choices are influenced by what source of authority we honor. When we choose God and His word as our authority, we will consult and consider what He says and what His desires are and form our decision in cooperation with Him. As we do this, we will have the faith of God to the degree we believe in our heart and speak what we believe. (Mark 11:22-23)

This is what Abraham began to learn while still in Harran. Abraham had to choose the authority forming his thoughts. We know when he heard God's words to him, he chose God. We have no idea if Abraham had ever heard God speak to him before or even if he knew the full story about God. It was possible, but we cannot assume he did. During King Josiah's reign (2Kings 22), the Book of the Law was found, and it was the first time Josiah had ever heard it read. Think of that– an Israelite king living in Jerusalem had never read the Torah! But when he heard it, it brought about revelation that changed the way he thought and ruled. Josiah's confidence in the Book of the Law and his resulting revelation and action brought blessing to him and to his people during his lifetime.

When Abraham first heard God's words, he made the decision to trust God. He did not limit himself by the circumstances of his birth, his marriage or what was expected of him by friends and neighbors. He did not allow a group of people who did not choose God to form his ideas of what was possible, what was right, what was his true identity and destiny.

If Abraham looked at his life, it didn't look good. His name was exalted father. It seemed an empty promise. His circumstances told him his wife could never have children. That was interpreted as a curse. But God's words told him something different, and Abraham got an invitation to a different destiny. "And I will make of you a great nation.

And I will bless you and make your name great; and you will be a blessing. And I will bless those who bless you, and curse the one despising you. And in you all families of the earth shall be blessed." (Genesis 12:2-3 LITV)

God promised to bless him not limit him. He would make him into a nation not just a family. Five times God assured Abraham of His will. Five times He said He would bless him. Abraham got a revelation: "God is the authority that blesses and He is the authority that can curse the curse cursing me."

Abraham chose wisely. God didn't force him because He doesn't make those kinds of decisions. He gave man the privilege of a free will. For example in the book of Esther, Esther was offered an invitation to cooperate with God to save the Israelites, but if she had refused, God would have found someone else who was willing. The Bible is filled with people who didn't choose God or cooperate with Him: Cain, Noah's neighbors, Pharaoh, King Saul and several Israelite kings, Jonah (at first), etc.

But Abraham allowed the hearing of God's word to become confidence, and he put his trust in God. When Abraham chose God as the Authority speaking into his life, he took God as the Lord of his life. His abundant life was about to begin.

Drawing Near Activity: Answer the questions below.

What forms your identity and determines your destiny? Why?

Why is it important to know what God says about you?

What is the place of faith?

Why is knowledge and admiration of God's word not considered faith?

How does faith come?

How does everyone operate on faith?

What was Abraham's revelation?

What does it mean to choose the authority speaking into your life?

Chapter 1 General Questions

1. Are people's names important? Why or why not?

Activity: For extra insight, read 1Chronicles 4:9-10 about Jabez. Did Jabez think his name could define him or his future? Why or why not? What does Jabez' experience tell you about God?

2. Explain what you learned about the term habiru.

3. What is the biblical definition of the word Hebrew?

4. What is important about the land of the *shasu*?

5. Why was the discovery of the Royal Archives in Ebla significant?

6. What do ancient words in the Bible suggest? (Ancient words like *mw* and *Kamāš*, for example.)

7. Compare King Ebrium of Ebla with Eber listed in Genesis 10.

8. Who were the Amorites?

9. Describe the ancient city of Mari.

10. What do the Mari Texts reveal about the Bible?

For further study:

"Your name is what gives you your soul."

Soul is "the vital force that animates the body and is the seat of the feelings, desires, affections and aversions...heart mind." (*Strong's Exhaustive Concordance* G5590 *psychē.*) It is the part of you we call the mind, will and emotions. The soul is one of the three parts forming man: man is a spirit; he has a soul and he lives in a body. (1 Thessalonians 5:23)

The soul is involved in helping us form our identity. With the will, we accept the thoughts our mind dwells on. The thoughts we choose to possess attach to us in the center of our being, lodging in what the Bible refers to as the heart. But the heart also thinks God tells us.

Proverbs 23:7 reveals the heart is the place where our true thoughts dwell. "For as he thinketh in his heart, so is he." Proverbs 4:23 tells us we are to guard our heart because out of it come the borders or "the place from which (any person or thing) goes forth." (*Strong's Exhaustive Concordance* H8444 *towtsa'ah.*)

What we believe to be true in the innermost part of ourselves forms our identity. It will determine what we choose to be possible and thus establish our destiny. While some well-meaning family member may have given us a name they thought appropriate, our ultimate destiny is up to us.

Jesus said it is out of the surplus of what a person has gathered in their heart that their mouth speaks. "A good man out of the good treasure of his heart bringeth forth that which is good; and an evil man out of the evil treasure of his heart bringeth forth that which is evil: for of the abundance of the heart his mouth speaketh." (Luke 6:45)

Our words express what are our values, opinions, dreams, goals, etc. But words can also penetrate our heart by a reverse action, which is why many cultures believe a name defines us. It is spoken often, and by hearing, it attaches to our thoughts and eventually lives in our heart. Certain words do the same for our identity and esteem.

Why do you think it is important to carefully choose the words you allow to attach to you?

Words are spiritual. They either speak life or death to you. The Bible tells us we are able to write them on our heart, and it encourages us to write God's words on our heart. "My son, keep my words, and lay up my commandments with thee. Keep my commandments, and live; and my law as the apple of thine eye. Bind them upon thy fingers, write them upon the table of thine heart." (Proverbs 7:1-3)

How do we write them on our heart? Our tongue writes. A Psalmist had thoughts bubbling up out of his heart and declared, "...my tongue is the pen of a ready (quick/skillful) writer." (Psalm 45:1)

This is not the power of positive speaking. Speaking positive words may feel good, but they are only spoken from the mind and may not be true. They might be enough to help you in the shallow waters of life, but they will never sustain you in deep water when the outcome is life or death to whatever you are facing.

Speaking God's words is powerful, however, because they are spirit and life Jesus said. "It is the spirit that quickeneth; the flesh profiteth nothing: the words that I speak unto you, they are spirit, and they are life." (John 6:63) God's words are Spirit because they are God breathed. "All Scripture is God-breathed and profitable for doctrine, for reproof, for correction, for instruction in righteousness, so that the man of God may be perfected, being fully furnished for every good work." (2Ti 3:16-17)

Read John 6:63 again. If your breath, your spirit, gives life to your flesh, your body, how much more would God's breath give life to you and in your circumstances?

Words are spoken thoughts. Thoughts come to us from two places: from our spirit to our soul or from an outside influence to our soul.[1] The outside influence is like the world's wisdom based on man's knowledge or from satan who tries to drop thoughts into our mind, hoping we will keep them and act them out. It is important to choose which ideas we hold on to and be sensitive to whether they agree with what God says about us or not. What we think on long enough, we believe, and what we believe, we eventually speak. Our voice is powerful in our ear.

Like Abraham, we have to choose the authority speaking into our life and the words we will write on our heart. We learned when Abraham heard God's words to him, he chose God and wrote His words on His heart.

Genesis 12:1-3 "Now the LORD had said unto Abram, Get thee out of thy country, and from thy kindred, and from thy father's house,

---

[1] Your spirit and soul work closely together. For more information read *Born Again: Not Just For Heaven* by Flying Eagle Publications.

unto a land that I will shew thee: And I will make of thee a great nation, and I will bless thee, and make thy name great; and thou shalt be a blessing: And I will bless them that bless thee, and curse him that curseth thee: and in thee shall all families of the earth be blessed."

The words Abraham chose to believe outlined his destiny. Notice that hearing God's words brought Abraham revelation. When he acted on this revelation, he became very different than his father, brother and nephew. The revelation brought faith, and this full persuasion resulted in an action.

Activity: Read 2Kings 22 and 23. When King Josiah heard the word of God read to him, it brought revelation and changed a nation.

Abraham's name had been Abram when he first heard God speak to him. Abram means exalted father. It was a name empty of promise since he could have no children. But God's words to him told him something different.

"I will bless," God said– not limit you.

"I will make you into a nation," God promised— not just a family. It was an invitation to a different destiny.

Drawing Near Activity: Quiet yourself and remove any distractions. Begin thanking God for being all that is good. Ask Him how He sees you. What words would He like to speak into your life?

Chapter Evaluation

Student may write what they learned from this chapter, using a paragraph essay format. Suggested: 500 words or one page. Alternative: Student may give an oral report or Charlotte Mason style narration. Or student may complete the test provided below.

Chapter 1 Test Questions

1. What do we know about the term habiru?

2. What is the biblical definition of the word Hebrew?

3. Why was the discovery of the Royal Archives in Ebla significant?

4. What do ancient words in the Bible like mw and Kamāš, suggest to us about the Bible?

5. Who was King Ebrium?

6. What biblical character do some scholars think King Ebrium may be?

7. Describe the Amorites.

8. What are some things we know about the ancient city of Mari?

9. What do the Mari Texts reveal about the Bible?

10. Was Abraham an Amorite? Why or why not?

Optional essay question: Why are names important? Give examples.

Chapter 2

Called Out From Ur

Devotion

Have your Bible, a journal and pen handy. Look up the verses quoted. Read them, the verses around them, and write down what you learn.

Not every Christian is called to remote deserts and isolated mountain ranges to serve God. Not every believer is assigned to urban or rural war zones. But all Christians are called. Being an electrician is a calling. Being a parent is a calling. Being a student, business owner, etc. is a calling.

All believers are expected to live out their lives in faithful dedication and in an intimate relationship with their Creator and Lord as a witness to their family and friends. And then there are those who are called to difficult places. Abraham was one of them.

God's first words to Abraham, "Get thee out of thy country, and from thy kindred, and from thy father's house, unto a land that I will shew thee," may not have enough details for the average Christian. What would you want God to add regarding the message if you were

Abraham? It is enough to wonder how Abraham knew Canaan was the destination. But we should not assume these were God's only words to Abraham. We are given what we need to know, and so probably was Abraham.

Abraham's calling included a separation from his old way of life. God wanted to do something brand new in Abraham. In a way it was like the old is gone part of our salvation as believers. When we take Jesus as our Lord, we are made brand new from the inside and our habits should reflect that. Jesus said we cannot put new wine in old wineskins. When we accept Jesus into our lives, it is time for us to analyze how our life patterns should change to honor Him.

When we become born again we are God's masterpiece. The inner change enables us to achieve good things– that is, if we allow it. Ephesians 2:10 says "For we are his workmanship, created in Christ Jesus unto good works, which God hath before ordained that we should walk in them." Workmanship is *poiēma,* a product. We are a product fabricated, *ktizō,* in Jesus to superimpose or to distribute, *epi,* good toil or deeds, *ergon,* that God fit up in advance, *proetoimazō,* in order that we should tread all around as proof of our ability and be occupied with them, *peripateō.*

Abraham struggled at times with these changes to do the good he was supposed to do. We see in him that change and this "workmanship" is a process. Even our calling is a process as we take one step, then another along the path God sets before us. The level of success we see is related to our obedience. We can delay or derail God's plans toward us according to our willingness to cooperate with Him.

Notice that God has prepared in advance everything needed to accomplish these good works. When He led the Israelites to the edge of the Red Sea and they saw they were hemmed in, it wasn't God who was in a panic. He had already prepared a way open for them to cross safely. The wind sent to reveal the path wasn't an omen of doom or for the purpose of added misery like they may have thought as they huddled on the shore.

When Abraham felt cornered during certain times of his life, he forgot to consider God's solutions. Like when he went to Egypt or settled near Abimelech or took Hagar as a concubine. We do not know how God would have delivered Abraham during those times because He wasn't given the chance. Thankfully Abraham was teachable and humble. While he may have messed up on occasion, Abraham never disobeyed what he understood to do. He was diligent to do the small things which led to the big things.

The small things are in front of all of us and most times they are only small to us. Abraham was building a life in Ur and in Harran. In Canaan, he would be a foreigner. But Abraham did two seemingly small things. He believed God would bless him, and he obeyed by taking one step then another toward Canaan. It was the beginning of things he never imagined could happen when he was still in his father's house.

Drawing Near Activity: Ask God to show you what habits or routines He would like to see eradicated from your life. Ask Him to tell you what skills or habits He would like to see strengthened or developed in you. Write them down and search for scriptures to encourage you in this process.

Chapter 2 General Questions

1. Describe the three Urs scholars consider may be linked to Abraham.

2. Name some important archaeological finds relating to each Ur.

Activity: Read a chapter or two of *Ninevah And Its Remains* by Sir Austen Henry Layard. The book can be read online at arhive.org. Use the link https://archive.org/details/ninevehanditsre03layagoog.

3. What is Agatha Christie's connection to the Sumerian city of Ur?

4. Describe the biblical Ur.

5. Describe what the Bible has to say about the Chaldeans or the *Kasdîy*.

6. What is the name of Abraham's homeland according to the Bible and in what modern countries is this region located today?

7. Why are the Nuzi Tablets important to the Genesis accounts?

8. Why were cities safer than the open country?

9. What pagan gods were worshipped in Ur?

10. Who was Henry Rawlinson?

11. Who was Iscah and what does Jewish tradition say concerning her?

12. Describe what we know about Abraham's family according to the Bible.

13. Why might Terah have decided to move to Canaan?

14. Why might Terah have "stopped" in Harran?

15. Define *yâshab*.

Activity: Draw a map of Mesopotamia and mark the three cities of Ur.

For further study:

It may be interesting to study the cylinder seal of Hašhamer, ensi of Iškun-Sin on the British Museum website. (The word *ensi* is translated governor.) The god Sin is represented by the crescent moon. The man sitting is the king, and it is thought that Hašhamer is the man being led to the king by the goddess Lamma.

Sometimes Sin is portrayed sitting on a winged bull in the form of an old man with a long beard. Actually his father was the bull. His name was Enil.

This god whom Abraham surely knew was worshipped throughout Mesopotamia and even into Arabia. Sin's name can be seen in many of the names from biblical times. For example, The Wilderness of Sin and Sennacherib. The temple in Harran was called house which gives joy, *E-hul-hul*. It is one of the temples the Babylonian king Nabonidas said he restored and mentions it on his Cylinder of Sippar. On the cylinder, Nabonidas tells the story of the moon god Sin being angry and commanding a king, Nabonidas, to restore his temple.

Restoring the temple, however, didn't help Nabonidas or his son, Bel-shar-usur better known as Belshazzar in the Bible (Daniel 5). Cyrus the Great would soon conquer the Babylonian Empire, leaving Belshazzar dead and Nabonidas dethroned. Of course Nabonidus lived hundreds of years after Abraham. But the god Sin lived as a pagan god long after Nabonidus or Abraham. The god was worshipped in the Middle East well into the Christian and Islamic period.

Archaeology has discovered many different idols from different locations, Qataban, Timna, Marib, Hazor, and in the countries of Syria, Iran, Iraq, Turkey and Egypt to name a few. The Bible mentions this type of worship several times in the Old Testament. In Deuteronomy 17:2-5, the Israelites are warned not to serve these false gods.

> If there be found among you, within any of thy gates which the LORD thy God giveth thee, man or woman, that hath wrought wickedness in the sight of the LORD thy God, in transgressing his covenant, And hath gone and served other gods, and worshipped them, either the sun, or moon, or any of the host of heaven, which I have not commanded; And it be told thee, and thou hast heard of it, and enquired diligently, and, behold, it be true, and the thing certain, that such abomination is wrought in Israel: Then shalt thou bring forth that man or that woman, which have committed that wicked thing, unto thy gates, even that man or that woman, and shalt stone them with stones, till they die.

The verse mentions the sun, moon and stars for a reason. Each had a pagan god named for them, a cult devoted to them, and a temple to honor them. They were a family of gods called a pantheon. Sin, the moon god, is also called Dilimbabbar or Ašimbabbar in some ancient literary texts as well as Suen and Nanna. His name was found in Ebla dating to 2400BC. Is Sin related to the family of gods Abraham's father and brother worshipped? The odds are good. Really good.

Why do you think the punishment for worshipping these gods among the Israelites was so severe?

Not many people worship the moon today by sacrificing animals, but astrology is a way of exalting the sun, moon and stars over God's word. Can you think of any other ways we might be toying with idol worship without realizing it?

The Bible says in 1Samuel 15:22-23 obedience is better than making religious sacrifices and pride is like idolatry. "And Samuel said, Does Jehovah delight in burnt offerings and sacrifices as in obeying the voice of Jehovah? Behold! Obeying is better than sacrifice; to give attention is better than the fat of rams. For the sin of divination is rebellion; insolence is both iniquity and idolatry." (LITV)

Insolence is pride. Pride can take many forms. God sees idolatry as pride because the person is honoring something unworthy over all God has done for them. There is a question many ask and think it is a puzzle to answer. Which came first the chicken or the egg? If you have a biblical worldview, your reply would be the chicken because God made all the birds, then they did bird things like laying eggs. This is what God says in Genesis 1. But if your worldview is influenced by evolution, your reply would be the egg, and you are left trying to explain how the egg formed.

Many people do not think the belief in God came first. They say all the pagan gods were first and people copied their religions to make up the Bible. This is not what the Bible says. God made man; man made other religions after he rebelled. And those idols? They are really evil spirits or demons. Here are three verses that confirm it.

> With strange gods they moved Him to jealousy; and with idols they provoked Him to anger. They sacrificed to demons who were not God, to gods whom they did not know, new ones who came lately. Your fathers had not dreaded them. You forgot the Rock that brought you into being and ceased to care for God who formed you. (Deut 32:16-18)
>
> And they served their idols, and they became a snare to them. Yea, they sacrificed their sons and their

daughters to the demons; and they shed innocent blood, the blood of their sons and of their daughters, whom they sacrificed to the idols of Canaan. And the land was polluted with the blood. (Psalm 106:36- 38 LITV)

What I say is that the things offered by the Gentiles are offered to evil spirits and not to God; and it is not my desire for you to have any part with evil spirits. It is not possible for you, at the same time, to take the cup of the Lord and the cup of evil spirits; (1 Corinthians 10:20-21 BBE)

To the degree we respect God's word as true, is the degree we honor God with obedience. To step away from God and what He says, no matter the distance, is to honor something else.

Drawing Near Activity: Take time to examine your relationship with God. Are there areas you may have stepped away from God and His way? Commit them to God and ask Him to strengthen you. Lean into Holy Spirit's power to help. You are not supposed to do this earth walk on your own. God called you out from where you were, your Ur, to be your Father, your Friend, the Lover of your life.

Chapter Evaluation

Student may write what they learned from this chapter, using a paragraph essay format. Suggested: 500 words or one page. Alternative: Student may give an oral report or Charlotte Mason style narration. Or student may complete the test provided below.

Chapter 2 Test Questions

1. Give a brief description of each Ur.

2. Name some important archaeological finds relating to each Ur.

3. What is the name and location of Abraham's homeland?

4. What is Agatha Christie's connection to the Sumerian city of Ur?

5. What does the Bible say about the Chaldeans or the *Kasdiy*?

6. According to the Bible, what do we know about Abraham's family?

7. Why are the Nuzi Tablets important to the Genesis accounts?

8. Why were cities safer than the open country?

9. What was the name of the city where Abraham stopped after leaving Ur?

10. Define *yâshab*.

Optional essay question: Which Ur may have the strongest biblical and archaeological evidence to be Abraham's Ur? Support your answer with scriptures and archaeological data.

Chapter 3

Canaan

Devotion

Have your Bible, a journal and pen handy. Look up the verses quoted. Read them, the verses around them, and write down what you learn.

In his 1828 *American Dictionary Of The English Language*, Noah Webster defines peace as "a state of quiet and freedom from disturbance or agitation" and this may apply to a society, an individual or to the "temper of the mind." He adds peace is freedom from "agitation or disturbance by the passions, as from fear, terror, anger, anxiety or the like." It is a "calmness" and "quiet of conscience."

Many think the only way to achieve this state of peace is to live isolated from other people and world events. They envision a remote retreat where they and a few chosen loved ones are able to survive without interruptions, agitations and disturbances from the outside world.

Christians like the idea of peace. We stand in the chaotic space we know as our life and when things get to be too much, we close our eyes and imagine heaven, the only place we think peace exists. We might not realize it, but this focusing and imagining is the key to peace. Fix our eyes on Jesus, the Bible tells us. Why? Because then we are not tormented with the world and its noise.

When Abraham left Harran at the word of God, he crossed the Euphrates and entered a land loud with sin. But wait– wasn't Harran full of idols? Whatever was in Harran apparently did not have the potential of Canaan's singleness for evil and rebellion. Abraham himself said there was no fear of God in the place (Genesis 20:11). God said He was going to judge Canaan. For whatever reason, He didn't include northern Mesopotamia at the same time.

As soon as Abraham arrived he began to fix his eyes. He built an altar in Canaan. Abraham didn't have the 23rd Psalm to read, but he may have felt like he was walking in the valley of the shadow of death. He was an alien, a well supplied one. Vulnerable. No family ties to the land. Immorality surrounded him. He was different and stood out from the Canaanites. But Abraham focused on the words God had spoken to him. Blessing. Protection. Mercy. So he built an altar and worshipped.

Psalm 23:5 says God sets in a row and arranges in order, *ârak*, a table for us in the midst of our enemies. " Thou preparest a table before me in the presence of mine enemies." Abraham trusted God had arranged to supply blessing, goodness and mercy for him in the middle of Canaan's evil. So Abraham sat at the table God provided.

Abraham never made any attempts to conform to the society surrounding him. He described himself as a stranger, *gêr*, and a foreigner, *tôshâb*. This was his spiritual identity as well. We read of only one family he befriended, Mamre's. We read of servants numbering into the hundreds willing to follow him into battle (Genesis 14) and one who knew how to pray (Genesis 24). And, we read of the building of several altars to the Lord wherever Abraham traveled.

Canaan was a lawless place, the place he was called to possess. Abraham understood peace was only going to come to him if it was first cultivated in his heart. The spiritual atmosphere around him depended on his perspective. So he focused on building altars, on calling upon the Lord and being obedient to God. He was living out Isaiah 26:3. "Thou wilt keep him in perfect peace, whose mind is stayed on thee: because he trusteth in thee."

Lot was with him all this time, but we never read about Lot building an altar when he moved to the plains east of the Jordan. Instead we read he was troubled at the sin in Sodom where he lived (2Peter 2:7). Vexed is the word used in some Bibles. Lot didn't have peace. He didn't have the motivation to separate himself, and he barely escaped death. (Genesis 19:16)

The area where Lot ended up was outside of Canaan proper. Was Abraham grieved Lot left the region of his blessing? Abraham tells us nothing of his thoughts.

Instead, Abraham teaches us it is possible to thrive in the middle of evil. But it depends who we surround ourselves with, what we are focused on and if we are willing to build our altar in Canaan and give God a place there.

Christians may complain about unbelieving co-workers, bosses or friends. We may complain about environments that ooze immorality. It is okay to assess the evil and judge it as such. But then what? To talk more about it magnifies it. To meditate on it steals your attention and focus. What do you do?

Build your altar in Canaan. Feed from the table God has given you to strengthen you. In the midst of evil, praise God. Repeat verses and pray them back to Him. Thank Him for the goodness and mercy and blessing that He has prepared for you in the presence of your enemies and that will be with you forever. Pray for those around you and watch what happens as you feed from the table the Lord has set for you.

Drawing Near Activity: What areas exist in your life or surroundings that trouble you? How can you worship God and give Him a place there? What praises can you offer? What verses could encourage you? Make a list and draw up a plan of action. When the anxiety strikes or the pressure closes in, remind yourself, God has provided a table of good things for you right there in the presence of your enemy. Start thanking Him!

Chapter 3 General Questions

1. Describe the city of Harran.

2. Where does Abraham's life story fit in our dates for history?

3. What belief or theory complicates dating biblical history?

4. What is the biblical total of years for man's history so far?

Activity: Research the evidence for a young earth. Which of the discoveries do you find most compelling?

5. What significant event happened at Hamoukar?

6. What are some reasons scholars give for why Terah might have wanted to move to Canaan?

7. Explain slavery in the Early Bronze Age.

Activity: Using the maps at the end of Chapters 1 and 2, plot the routes Abraham may have taken from Harran into Canaan.

8. Define Moreh.

9. Why is Moreh an important site?

10. What city was later built near Moreh?

11. What are two events that happened in Shechem that link the Old Testament to the New Testament?

12. What does Bethel mean?

13. What did Abraham begin to do between the cities of Bethel and Ai?

14. Describe what Abraham's tents and camp may have looked like.

15. How did Abraham think of himself?

16. What did a Syrian farmer discover by accident?

17. Did the Canaanite tablets found at Ras Shamra, Syria, confirm what the Bible said about Canaanite culture?

18. What two religions are connected to Abraham?

19. What problem did Abraham face soon after entering Canaan?

20. How could the ancient Middle East have supported the large flocks and herds represented in the Bible?

21. What did Abraham decide to do to solve the problem he faced after arriving in Canaan?

22. What did Abraham think his next problem was going to be in going to Egypt?

23. What was his solution?

24. What happened to Sarah because of Abraham's solution?

Drawing Near Activity: God has promised that He will guide His people. But He is looking for our cooperation. James 1:5 says that when we ask for wisdom, God will answer without scolding us. This mercy was as available to Abraham as it is to us.

Today we can be led by Holy Spirit whom Jesus sent to be our Guide, our Teacher and source of Wisdom. He never overrides your decisions. He will allow you to make a mistake if you insist upon it. That is why it is important to be in close relationship with God, so close that you depend on Him to make the smallest decisions as well as the big ones.

Quiet yourself and remove any distractions. Make a firm decision to take Jesus as your Lord, the One who has the power and the authority in your life, and depend on Him to lead you along your way. Ask Holy Spirit to teach you how to be sensitive to His voice so you know God's will concerning the decisions you have to make.

Chapter Evaluation

Student may write what they learned from this chapter, using a paragraph essay format. Suggested: 500 words or one page. Alternative: Student may give an oral report or Charlotte Mason style narration. Or student may complete the test provided below.

Chapter 3 Test Questions

1. Where does Abraham's life story fit in our dates for history?

2. Why is Moreh an important site?

3. What is the biblical total of years for man's history so far?

4. What was slavery like in the Early Bronze Age?

5. Did the Canaanite tablets found at Ras Shamra, Syria, confirm what the Bible said about Canaanite culture? Why or why not?

6. What two religions are connected to Abraham?

7. What problem did Abraham face soon after entering Canaan?

8. How could the ancient Middle East have supported the large flocks and herds represented in the Bible?

9. What did Abraham decide to do to solve his problem soon after he arrived in Canaan?

10. What did Abraham think his next problem was going to be in going to Egypt?

Optional essay question: Compare the city of Harran with the land of Canaan.

Chapter 4

The Egypt Incident

Devotion

Have your Bible, a journal and pen handy. Look up the verses quoted. Read them, the verses around them, and write down what you learn.

The Bible tells us love is not selfish. Sarah certainly could teach us about that couldn't she? The lawlessness of Canaan made an impression on Sarah and Abraham. Abraham feared for his life. Not because of robbers and thieves but because of beauty. Sarah was beautiful and men noticed. Ambrose Bierce defined beauty as the power by which a woman charms a lover and terrifies a husband.[1]

And Abraham was scared. He worried someone would kill him so they could marry her. You might laugh when you realize Sarah was in her sixties. But hey, it happened. Even when she was ninety, it wasn't her young maid Hagar that caught the king's eye. It was Sarah. We all want to see Sarah in heaven, don't we?

Anyway Abraham asked Sarah a favor. Probably no woman today

---

[1] Ambrose Bierce Quotes. BrainyQuote.com, BrainyMedia Inc, 2022. https://www.brainyquote.com/quotes/ambrose_bierce_162731,

would ever agree to this promise but it is likely no woman would be in her situation today either. Abraham had asked if she would tell the Canaanites she was his sister. He reminded her of this as they traveled to Egypt. "Please say that you are my sister, so that it may be well with me for your sake, and my soul shall live because of you." (LITV)

We read this and cringe at the sacrifice he is asking of Sarah. "So that it will be well with me." What about her? It was for her sake, he said. But God didn't ask this of Sarah; Abraham did. Abraham explained to Abimelech, "And it came to pass, when God caused me to wander from my father's house, that I said unto her, This is thy kindness which thou shalt shew unto me; at every place whither we shall come, say of me, He is my brother." (Genesis 20:13)

Abraham's request was born out of fear. Sarah did offer this kindness to him but what was offered her? She was now on the open market, and she was taken twice. Thankfully God saved her both times, but what a racket these two were plying around Canaan. Having no children made the deception easy. Children, however, at least a son, was what they both wanted.

In the Bible, seeking help from Egypt was never a good idea. It came at a cost. When we are in the wrong place in life, it costs us. When we rely on our own wisdom, it can have the opposite result we intended.

When Sarah agreed to the deception Abraham offered, she lost her identity as his wife. In Genesis 17:5, 19 and 18:9-10, the Lord reminded Abraham that Sarah was his wife. Did he need a reminder? Did she? Not that they weren't together, but what was their perception of each other? Of Sarah about herself? The Lord corrected the deception.

When we are in the wrong place, either out of God's will on purpose or by mistake, our identity suffers. We forget who we are and what is important. Relationships are affected. Our future is in danger.

Disobedience steals. When we stray knowingly or unknowingly we are vulnerable to these attacks because we have an enemy only too willing to take advantage. "Be sober, be vigilant; because your adversary the devil, as a roaring lion, walketh about, seeking whom he may devour." (1Peter 5:8)

Pressure can be subtle. It can come from someone you love and respect. But the source may be fear. It is dangerous to make decisions based on fear. We are to cast our cares on God. He did not give us a Spirit of fear.

Abraham thought he was acting wisely. He was acting on his *fears*. There was real danger in Canaan, yes, but we will never know how Abraham, with God's help, could have handled it otherwise.

Drawing Near Activity: Determine not make decisions based on fear. Ask the Holy Spirit to identify any areas of fear and fear based decisions in your life. The process of making decisions matters. Always take the time to consult God even in the smallest of things like what to eat, where to shop for groceries, what show to watch. When you are in the habit of asking His counsel for the little things, you won't forget to ask His advice in the big things. This week practice asking.

Chapter 4 General Questions

1. Do you think Abraham made a mistake when he went to Egypt? Why or Why not?

2. What do you think might have been the hardest part of the situation in Egypt for Sarah to deal with? Explain your answer.

3. The incident that involved Sarah, Abraham and Pharaoh in Egypt foreshadows what later event in Israel's history?

4. Why does the Bible say Abraham and Sarah "went up" out of Egypt?

For Further Study:

When you hear about the riches of ancient Egypt, you may wonder what those treasures were and how they would compare to our idea of wealth today. Actually, they would still be considered valuable. Gold, unlike cowrie shells, wampum or whale teeth, is still making people rich.

Egypt had gold. While there may be only one mine in operation there today since oil is more in demand, Nubia's ancient name *nbw* meant gold. Among the first writings of hieroglyphs in the Early Dynastic Period are pictures of collars standing in for the word gold.

But archaeologists have discovered gold jewelry they believe predates the first pharaohs. Some of this gold has silver in it, so we know both were possible to obtain during Abraham's lifetime as the Bible tells us he was rich in both. "And Abram was very rich in cattle, in silver, and in gold." (Genesis 13:2)

The Nile River was also a source of wealth because it brought dark soil from deep Africa and deposited it in Egypt when the river flooded its banks every year. As the Egyptians learned to deal with the flooding, a rich agricultural system developed and farmers grew crops like wheat, flax, barley and onions.

Egypt did have famines but it remained a place to retreat to in case of one it seems. Why do you think the people of Canaan were tempted to travel to Egypt during hard times?

The Bible makes many references to what we know as the Egyptian Empire. Most of them are bad. Why do you think this is so? Read Isaiah 19:1-25; Isaiah 31:1; Revelation 11:8. Compare these passages and write down the descriptive words.

5. Describe the Negev.

6. What is the controversy over Abraham's camels?

7. How is the controversy solved?

8. To what Canaanite cities did Abraham return to after he left Egypt?

9. Explain who the Canaanites were.

10. Write God's covenant with Abraham in your own words.

11. What is the importance of God's promises to Abraham and are they valid today?

12. Describe the situation with Lot.

13. What are your thoughts concerning Lot's choice?

14. How did Abraham's kindness to Lot prove his trust in God?

15. In what way(s) did God encourage Abraham?

Drawing Near Activity: Acts 20:35 is often quoted, it is more blessed to give than receive, when we need to remind ourselves we don't need to get a gift in return. But God is never in the business of not rewarding in some way our obedience to give. When Abraham acted on his trust in God by giving to Lot, God wanted to reward Abraham's trust—not because He had to but because God is good. He acts in love toward us.

Never be afraid to give to God. When you give God anything– the small things and the bigger things like your future, your life, your health, your relationships– He is able to give back to you with abundance. The key is trust. You must not allow fear to take the place of your trust or to elevate itself above God's word to you.

Abraham had a promise from God. What promise has He given you? It is time to ask Him.

Get your Bible, your journal and a pen that works. Then find a quiet place and draw near to Him. Begin to praise Him and thank Him for His love. Ask Him to lead you to His promises for you. Write them down. Memorize them. Let these promises of pure love replace your hesitancy to give to God or others. Then watch for an opportunity to act out your trust.

Chapter Evaluation:

Student may write what they learned from this chapter, using a paragraph essay format. Suggested: 500 words or one page. Alternative: Student may give an oral report or Charlotte Mason style narration. Or student may complete the test provided below.

Chapter 4 Test Questions

1. What happened to Sarah and Abraham in Egypt?

2. The incident that involved Sarah, Abraham and Pharaoh in Egypt foreshadows what later event in Israel's history?

3. Why does the Bible say Abraham and Sarah "went up" out of Egypt?

4. Describe the Negev.

5. What is the controversy over Abraham's camels?

6. How is the controversy solved?

7. Who were the Canaanites and what were they like?

8. What was included in God's covenant with Abraham?

9. Who was Lot and what was the situation between him and Abraham?

10. How did Abraham's kindness to Lot prove his trust in God?

Optional essay question: What is the importance of God's promises to Abraham and are they valid today?

Chapter 5

The Not So Legendary Battle of Siddim

Devotion

Have your Bible, a journal and pen handy. Look up the verses quoted. Read them, the verses around them, and write down what you learn.

    Someone has said on the topic of success that you should fake it until you make it. Over three hundred male servants born into Abraham's household were about to find out if Abraham was faking when he said God would bless him and curse those who cursed him.

    Abraham had some fantastic promises from God. He was promised a country and that God would make him into a nation. The land may not have been a grand size, but most of us would have been happy with all A's in math or an increase in our paycheck.

    God told Abraham he would make his name great, *gâdal*, to magnify, to increase, to make large, and honor. He said Abraham would be a blessing to all the people on earth. Those not captured by Chedorlaomer were just hoping he was going to be a blessing to them by rescuing their family members.

    Mamre, Eshcol and Aner were bound by a covenant with Abraham. They too went with Abraham to pursue Chedorlaomer and his kingly allies. But no one from the attacked cities is recorded going with him. No one else from Canaan besides the three brothers. Were they wondering if their mission would bring them death?

We do not know. But Abraham must have portrayed such confidence and ability because no one wavered. This is what Abraham is famous for. Not that he kicked the daylights out of Chedorlaomer's forces and brought back captives and spoils. Abraham is famous for *not wavering*. He didn't go back and forth between his opinions. He never withdrew his confession. He never doubted that God could be trusted or that He was good. Romans 4:20-21 says, "He staggered not at the promise of God through unbelief; but was strong in faith, giving glory to God; And being fully persuaded that, what he had promised, he was able also to perform."

There are over 3,000 promises God has announced in the Bible. Do any of them make you stagger? There is even a promise that all the promises are yes and amen, meaning God will honor them now. "For all the promises of God in him are yea, and in him Amen, unto the glory of God by us." (2Corinthians 1:20) We bring God glory when we know those promises and put our confidence in them, praising Him for His love and mercy toward us.

Abraham is still bringing God glory when we read how he acted on those promises and trusted God, never wavering. It was a process for Abraham to receive all God's promises in every area of his life, but he was well on his way into the journey of faith.

Drawing Near Activity: Are you willing to be taught what the word says or do you settle for what tradition says it means? The Pharisees in

Jesus' day knew the word well, but they were not open to what it really meant. Jesus wanted to show them but they were not willing.

Abraham was willing to learn what he didn't know. He was willing to enter new territory and expand his experience with God. Where are you on your journey? Are you hindering yourself by not allowing the Holy Spirit of God to counsel you and teach you? Ask God to help you understand where you are concerning this important crossroad in your life.

Chapter 5 General Questions:

1. Explain what we know about the city of Bethel.

2. Describe Hebron and why it is an important place for Israelis and Christians.

3. What were the names of Abraham's friends living near Hebron?

4. Who was Chedorlaomer and why did he want to go to Canaan?

5. What is the controversy over the kings in Genesis 14?

6. Who is T.G. Pinches and why is he important to our study of Genesis 14?

7. Read Genesis 14 for yourself. Name the four kings allied with Chedorlaomer, and then list the five kings from the cities on the plain.

8. Briefly describe Chedorlaomer's campaign and the fate of the people living in or near the cities on the plain.

9. Explain the geography of the land around the Dead Sea.

10. Who is David Ben-Gad Cohen and what is important to Bible believing Christians about his research?

11. How do the excavations at En Gedi and Dr. Osgood's research relate to Genesis 14?

12. How did Abraham find out Lot had been taken captive?

13. What did Abraham do in response to the news?

Activity: Look at the map at the end of Chapter 1. Do you think it was possible for Elamite kings to have ruled in Sumerian cities?

Sometimes we think of ancient people in segregated bubbles, this empire or culture then that one with no overlap as if boundaries were walls. This was not true in many places on the earth and certainly not in Mesopotamia. Name five facts, biblical or archaeological, that prove this concerning our study of Abraham.

14. Why is the word *chânîyk* important?

15. Who was Melchizedek?

16. What does Eli Shukron think he has discovered in Jerusalem?

17. Why do you think Abraham would not accept gifts or payment from the ruler of Sodom?

18. What was the spiritual importance of Abraham defending the people of Canaan?

19. What insight does King Suppiluliuma give us?

20. Do you believe there is enough biblical and archaeological evidence to solve the controversies of Genesis 14?

For further study:
When God calls us to a career, a ministry, or task, we need to remind ourselves He has gone before us to prepare and to equip us for whatever will be needed. But He expects us to access it by trusting Him to provide and perform.

Many verses in the Bible advise us to lay hold, to hold onto, to cleave unto. In Paul's letter to the Philippians, 3:12 says, "...but I press on, if I also may lay hold, inasmuch as I also was laid hold of by Christ Jesus." (LITV) When Jesus lays hold of us, *katalambanō*, He seizes us for His purpose. This is what Paul is saying happened to him. Jesus laid hold of him to preach the Good News to the Gentiles.

But notice what else Paul is saying. He declares he is seizing Jesus; he is laying hold of Him. This is the only way to be successful in life's callings, whether you are a student, a mom, a factory worker, a nurse or a missionary.

How do we take hold? We press on. We remain faithful, trusting God by thinking on His words to us, casting our fears and cares on Him, trusting Him to supply our every need. We never separate ourselves from Him in word or deed.

When Abraham set out for Canaan, God knew he would face opposition. He knew there would be enemies. It is why God equipped him with blessing, and it is why He promised to defend him. He does the same for us. It is our job to stay close to Him, listening and then doing what He tells us without delay.

Drawing Near Activity: Ask God to show you what He is calling you to lay hold of. Write down what He tells you. Then write a letter to yourself declaring how you will remain faithful and press on. What will you do? What will you say to remind yourself to give God your cares and fears and fully trust in Him?

Chapter Evaluation

Student may write what they learned from this chapter, using a paragraph essay format. Suggested: 500 words or one page. Alternative: Student may give an oral report or Charlotte Mason style narration. Or student may complete the test provided below.

Chapter 5 Test Questions

1. Describe Hebron and why it is an important place for Israelis and Christians.

2. What was the spiritual importance of Abraham defending the people of Canaan?

3. What does Eli Shukron think he has discovered in Jerusalem?

4. Who was Melchizedek?

5. Who was Chedorlaomer and why did he want to go to Canaan?

6. What is the controversy over the kings in Genesis 14?

7. Who is T.G. Pinches and why is he important to our study of Genesis 14?

8. Who is David Ben-Gad Cohen and what is important to Bible believing Christians about his research?

9. Why is the word *chânîyk* important?

10. How do the excavations at En Gedi and Dr. Osgood's research relate to Genesis 14?

Optional essay question: Briefly describe Chedorlaomer's campaign, its effect concerning the people living in or near the cities on the plain and Abraham's response.

Chapter 6

Making Abraham

Devotion

Have your Bible, a journal and pen handy. Look up the verses quoted. Read them, the verses around them, and write down what you learn.

When a person prays to God, most of the time they are not thinking about how they may cooperate with God. They are thinking all that pertains to their request is up to God and at His discretion. If what they wanted doesn't happen, they assume God has said no. But that isn't what we see Abraham thinking. Why?

He had a firm promise from God that his descendants would inherit the land of Canaan. Abraham never gave up on God's word that this was His will. Abraham took God at His word, is one way to say it. In Genesis 15, we read that Abraham was asking God where was the promised kid to start the ball rolling.

Abraham had been in Canaan for ten years. He and Sarah had diligently been trying to have a baby, but so far they rated a big fat zero. Abraham repeated the promise back to God. God reassured him that he would have a child.

Abraham believed and the Bible said it was credited to him as righteousness. Abraham asked for a contract of sorts concerning his inheriting the land when he said, "Lord GOD, whereby shall I know that I shall inherit it?" (Genesis 15:8) But he didn't ask any more details about having a son.

God gave Abraham what he asked for and a bit more information about his family's future. In fact, God never withheld anything from Him. We might assume if he would have asked for wisdom about his promised son, God would have provided it.

We have no evidence that Abraham told Sarah about all this, but soon after, Sarah marched out Hagar and offered her to Abraham, which was a custom in the cultures around them. It was not, however, what God intended. Look at the wording in Genesis 16:2. "And Sarai said unto Abram, Behold now, the LORD hath restrained me from bearing: I pray thee, go in unto my maid; it may be that I may obtain children by her. And Abram hearkened to the voice of Sarai."

From this verse we understand Sarah blamed God for her barrenness and decided she would never have a child. She did not believe God had chosen her to be the promised son's mother. It had been ten years in Canaan. Over five back in Aram-naharaim. She wasn't waiting any longer.

But the next words are very important. "And Abram hearkened to the voice of Sarai." Notice that he didn't hearken to the voice of God.

Hearken is *shâma*, to hear intelligently with the notion to obey. Hearken in English means to listen with respect or to heed. It is nice Abraham showed her respect, but this was reasoning based on their own knowledge, a conclusion based on the circumstances. It was a counterfeit word given to them to produce a counterfeit heir.

Sarah may have thought she was cooperating with God by surrendering. But cooperating with God is allowing yourself to be led by

Making Abraham

His Holy Spirit and the words He gives to you.[1] God's plan from the beginning involved Abraham and Sarah.

Cooperating with God is holding fast to the promise He gives you. Hebrews 10:23 says, "Let us hold fast the profession of our faith without wavering; (for he is faithful that promised." This verse closely resembles what was said of Abraham in Romans 4:20-21. It says, "He staggered not at the promise of God through unbelief; but was strong in faith, giving glory to God; And being fully persuaded that, what he had promised, he was able also to perform." While Abraham trusted God for provision first, eventually he got to this point of cooperation concerning his promised son.

God intends that as believers we walk by faith, not by sight. Sight is what we see happening, the circumstances we are in. Instead we are to walk, to go ahead, to proceed on the path in trust toward the outcome God has set in place for us.

Hebrews 10:35-38 outlines how to cooperate with God once you know His will for you. "Cast not away therefore your confidence, which hath great recompence of reward. For ye have need of patience, that, after ye have done the will of God, ye might receive the promise. For yet a little while, and he that shall come will come, and will not tarry. Now the just shall live by faith: but if any man draw back, my soul shall have no pleasure in him."

Patience is *hupomonē*, cheerful constancy and endurance. It derives from the word *hypomenō*, to remain or abide. It means you must not go ahead on your own, but remain cheerfully, in constancy, in endurance with the word given you. This is your confession of faith, for salvation, for healing, for deliverance.

---

[1] For more on how to be led by the Spirit, read *How To Walk In The Spirit* by Flying Eagle Publications.

It is interesting that while Abraham gave Sarah respect, disrespect from Hagar is what Sarah would reap, and Abraham too since Hagar would run away from them both. Abraham and Sarah had disrespected God by not bringing their idea before Him for His counsel. We must be on guard for the counterfeit, the seemingly good idea, the words spoken to us by friends, etc. or the counterfeit opportunities offered to us.

Drawing Near Activity: When what you have asked for hasn't arrived but you know God desires to give it to you, it is okay to ask Him to show you the reason. Refrain from blaming. Perhaps you are stuck in unbelief in a way you are not aware of. Sarah had at least five years of discouragement before Canaan to deal with. Her expectancy meter suffered. Is yours? Ask God to reveal your measure of expectancy. Thank Him for the wisdom He gives you and determine to do what He says.

Hupomonē is a cheerful constancy and endurance. This is a time to praise and be thankful for all God is working on your behalf. Praise is faith in God's goodness and character. Waiting is not a time to draw back. It is the time to possess! Thank Him for your answer and imagine yourself enjoying it. No matter how long it takes…

Chapter 6 General Questions

1. What bothered Abraham?

2. How did God encourage him?

3. Did Abraham understand God's encouragement? Explain your answer.

4. What was Abraham's "vision" problem? What did he struggle to "see" ?

5. Describe how his uncertainty fed his fear.

6. Define blind faith.

7. Does God require us to have blind faith? Why or why not?

8. In your own words, what is the biblical definition of faith?

Activity: Compare fear and faith. Define both. Using a topical index, Bible dictionary or even Google, find verses that deal with both. Jesus told Jairus to fear not. Did He say this to others? Why? The Bible says in 2Timothy 1:7 that God did not give us a spirit of fear. Where do you think fear comes from and what is its purpose? Did fear help Abraham? Identify any areas in your life where you are exhibiting fear and give those places to God. We are able to bring our thoughts into obedience to Jesus and to cast down our imagination when it wanders into fear. (Read 2Corinthians 10:5)

9. Why is imagination important to faith?

10. What is the archaeological evidence for making a servant an heir?

11. Read the fourth chapter of Romans. Why did God grant righteousness to Abraham?

12. Why is this imputation of righteousness significant to us and to the concept of grace through faith in Ephesians 2:8? "For by grace are ye saved through faith; and that not of yourselves: it is the gift of God."

Activity: Beginning in Genesis 12, read all the conversations between God and Abraham. What conclusions can you make about God?

13. Briefly outline what a blood covenant is, its importance, and how it was used in Abraham's day.

14. What details did God give Abraham during their encounter in Genesis 15?

15. What seems to have happened in Sarah's life during this time and what did she do to "solve" it?

16. Is there archaeological evidence of such a custom as Sarah chose?

17. Describe Hagar and her reaction to her promotion in Abraham's household.

18. What was Sarah's response to Hagar's abuse? Do you think Sarah was harsh? Why or why not?

19. How do we know Abraham and Sarah did not make the right choices concerning Hagar?

20. Why was Abraham's obedience critical when he was ninety-nine?

21. Why did God change their names?

22. What did God tell Abraham to do as a sign of his part of the covenant? State the archaeological evidence of this practice.

23. What made Abraham laugh when God was talking to him?

24. How do we know Abraham either did not understand or did not accept what God was telling him about Sarah?

25. Describe the Lord's visit to Abraham and Sarah in Genesis 18.

Drawing Near Activity: What promise or desire have you cast aside, given up on or declared impossible? Dust it off and place it in the Lord's hands. Ask Him to tell you about it and what to do about it. Write down what He says. If it is a yes, start praising Him for going ahead of you and providing favor and open doors for you. If it is a no, ask Him to give you a desire. Then start praising Him for going ahead of you and providing favor and open doors.

Write your faith projects down where you will see them everyday and thank Him for bringing them to pass in your life.

Chapter Evaluation

Student may write what they learned from this chapter, using a paragraph essay format. Suggested: 500 words or one page. Alternative: Student may give an oral report or Charlotte Mason style narration. Or student may complete the test provided below.

Chapter 6 Test Questions

1. What bothered Abraham after he returned from rescuing Lot?

2. What was Abraham's "vision" problem?

3. In your own words, what is the biblical definition of faith?

4. Why is imagination important to faith?

5. What is the archaeological evidence for making a servant an heir?

6. What details did God give Abraham during their encounter in Genesis 15?

7. What seems to have happened in Sarah's life during this time and

what did she do to "solve" it?

8. Is there archaeological evidence of such a custom as Sarah chose?

9. What did God tell Abraham to do as a sign of his part of the covenant? State the archaeological evidence of this practice.

10. Why was Abraham's obedience critical when he was ninety-nine?

Optional essay question: How do we know Abraham and Sarah did not make the right choices concerning Hagar? Or, In your own words, what is the biblical definition of faith?

Chapter 7

Sodom and Ishmael: Paying the Piper

Devotion

Have your Bible, a journal and pen handy. Look up the verses quoted. Read them, the verses around them, and write down what you learn.

 Believers in Jesus don't always start out in obedient Christian families with a legacy of devotion to God. Even if they do, they screw it up along the way because of some dumb decision they made. Big or small, we all have a few things we'd like to do over or just NOT do.
 We wonder if Lot had to do it all over again if he would have moved into Sodom. Lot never had to make big decisions for much of his life. He coasted in the shadow of Abraham's blessing and integrity toward God. He was never required to do the big things on his own.
 But then there comes a time when your path turns and you are on your own. It is time they say to put your big boy pants on and grow up. This usually happens at the same time pressures close in from outside sources. It is decision time.
 One day Lot was living in Canaan. Then he wasn't. One day Lot was tending his large flocks and herds. Then he wasn't. He was living in

a house in town– just like the rest of the nomadic shepherds. He had chosen a different lifestyle than Abraham's and that life looked a lot like the world's.

Not that Lot gave up on God or what was moral. He just didn't do hard things like running to the mountains when two angels told him to run for his life. Lot liked compromise. He settled for small. Compromise is a way of making an agreement where both parties surrender something desired to stop a disagreement. It can work. Or it can be a very bad idea.

When Lot was pressured to surrender the angels to the wicked crowd milling outside his house, Lot offered a compromise. His daughters. But compromising with evil shouldn't happen. We have to guard our words at times like these. It is better to stay silent. Lot lost everything except his daughters, who, ended up using him as their compromise.

Lot had made some decisions that probably seemed good to him at the time, but what he was doing is what the Bible calls sowing to the flesh. He was led by his senses, what he could see, feel, hear and reason on his own. Abraham did this too with the Hagar situation. Sarah's offer seemed good. It was smart, reasonable, and he really needed a kid. He and Sarah unknowingly rebelled against God's plan and birthed a "wild donkey" of a child. (Genesis 16:12) None of these actions were led by the Spirit of God, however.

There is a principle stated in Galatians 6:7 that says what a man sows he will reap. If you plant potatoes, you get potatoes. It is a version of "with the measure you use it will be measured to you." (Matthew 7:2) But Galatians 6:8 tells us a bit more of what we can expect about a person sowing and reaping. "For he that soweth to his flesh shall of the flesh reap corruption; but he that soweth to the Spirit shall of the Spirit reap life everlasting."

When Sarah, Abraham and Lot sowed to their flesh, they did the easy thing and never consulted God. They got corruption as their harvest, and they had to deal with the mess they made. Oh but thank God for His mercy! It is new every morning. Lot was called righteous in the New Testament. Sarah and Abraham miraculously received their promised son.

Drawing Near Activity: When you mess up, the hardest thing to do may be to forgive yourself. But focusing on your sin keeps you from experiencing all that Jesus won for you on the cross. You are free from condemnation. "There is therefore now no condemnation to them which are in Christ Jesus, who walk not after the flesh, but after the Spirit." (Romans 8:1)

You are free if you are in Jesus and walking after Holy Spirit. Allow God to speak His words over you about that incident. Are you keeping the door open to the enemy, satan, to accuse you? Ask God to give you His perspective of the whole thing. Notice any emotions triggered by the memories and surrender them to God.

Thank God for His mercy and forgiveness. Determine to live in the victory Jesus won for you on the cross.

Chapter 7 General Questions

1. Skeptics of the Bible think the account of Lot in the Bible was copied from Ovid's poem. Ovid was a Greek writer born about 43BC. Why is the skeptics' theory impossible even by their own dating method?

2. Why was the Lord on His way to Sodom?

3. What was Sodom famous for?

4. One of Sodom's sins was an abundance of idleness. The Hebrew word translated idleness is *shâqat*. What does it mean?

5. God promised Abraham He would spare the city if how many people were found to be righteous?

6. Where does the Bible say the five cities on the plain are located?

7. List the faults of Dr. Steven Collins' theory concerning the location for Sodom.

8. Why is Zoar important in the search for Sodom and what does archaeology and ancient literature have to say about the city?

9. How do the Ebla Tablets help scholars locate the five cities?

10. What two modern places are thought to be the ancient ruins of Sodom and Gomorrah?

11. Describe the archaeological discoveries at Sodom and Gomorrah.

12. What do geologists and archaeologist Bryant Wood believe to be the immediate cause of the destruction of the cities?

13. Do you think there is enough evidence to come to this conclusion?

14. Was there evidence at Sodom and Gomorrah of an earlier attack like the one Chedorlaomer carried out against these cities?

15. What is the evidence that Philistines were in Canaan during Abraham's lifetime?

16. What is the difference between Philistines and Phoenicians?

17. Describe the volatile situation with Ishmael and Hagar.

18. How do we know from the Bible that Ishmael's actions toward Isaac were not innocent?

19. What does "breaking the clump" mean?

20. How did the consequences of Abraham's choices affect him, Sarah, Isaac, Hagar and Ishmael?

21. Do you think Sarah's response to the situation was justified? Why or why not?

22. How was God kind to Ishmael? To Hagar?

Activity: How might you have tried to solve this family squabble? Try to think how your solution would have played out five years later. Do you think any scenario other than full control would have satisfied Ishmael and Hagar? Why or why not?

23. What does *châmâs* mean?

Activity: Research and read news articles and headlines happening in Israel and the Middle East today. Do you see any examples of *châmâs* today? Make a list of things to pray for to help the people of the Middle East settle their differences.

24. Why do we say Ishmael was "born of the flesh?"

25. What comparisons can you draw between Ishmael and Hagar and blended families? What would you say to Ishmael to help him and to encourage or comfort him?

Drawing Near Activity: Think of a time when your choices led to a consequence or affected others. Write it out and then ask God to forgive you for this situation. Or, maybe someone else's choices have negatively affected you. Write a prayer forgiving them. Analyze any emotions connected to these circumstances and surrender them to God. Don't forget to forgive yourself. Abraham eventually had the opportunity to bless Ishmael. Is there any action you can take to move forward from these sad memories?

Chapter Evaluation:

Student may write what they learned from this chapter, using a paragraph essay format. Suggested: 500 words or one page. Alternative: Student may give an oral report or Charlotte Mason style narration. Or student may complete the test provided below.

Chapter 7 Test Questions

1. Why was the Lord on His way to Sodom?

2. How do we know from the Bible that Ishmael's actions toward Isaac were not innocent?

3. What is the evidence that Philistines were in Canaan during Abraham's lifetime?

4. How did the consequences of Abraham's choices affect him, Sarah, Isaac, Hagar and Ishmael?

5. Why do we say Ishmael was "born of the flesh?"

6. Where does the Bible say the five cities on the plain are located?

7. The Hebrew word translated idleness is *shâqat*. What does it mean?

8. How do the Ebla Tablets help scholars locate the five cities?

9. What two modern places are thought to be the ancient ruins of Sodom and Gomorrah?

10. Was there evidence at Sodom and Gomorrah of an earlier attack like the one Chedorlaomer carried out against these cities? Explain your answer.

Optional essay question: Why is Zoar important in the search for Sodom and what does archaeology and ancient literature have to say about the city?

Chapter 8

The Binding of Isaac

Devotion

Have your Bible, a journal and pen handy. Look up the verses quoted. Read them, the verses around them, and write down what you learn.

The Binding of Isaac is a troubling story for many. How could God ask for child sacrifice when He considered it vile when practiced by others?

Abraham didn't know he was acting out a story God would use to teach about His Son. Abraham had made a covenant with God, and as a covenant partner and the father of our faith, he was the obvious choice to have his obedience tested.

The test was this: would Abraham withhold his son from God? The answer was no, with some unusual twists. Abraham never thought he would be returning home without Isaac. He believed God would provide a lamb. God did indeed provide, because what Abraham did not withhold from God, God would not withhold from him. He gave him Jesus.

It is a strange miraculous story, but then so is the cross. It is wonderfully strange in that no other has done for us what God has done, and He did it because He loves us. He was the only One who could accomplish our complete victory. And He wanted to– despite all we've done.

Abraham's head was probably swimming with thoughts as he descended that mountain. He had performed something unheard of and passed the test full of faith and hope. Can you imagine his thoughts as he looks at Jesus and ponders His wounds? Thankful is one. One day we will all be gathered around Jesus, looking upon Him as He sits on His throne, and all we will do is praise.

"After this I beheld, and, lo, a great multitude, which no man could number, of all nations, and kindreds, and people, and tongues, stood before the throne, and before the Lamb, clothed with white robes, and palms in their hands; And cried with a loud voice, saying, Salvation to our God which sitteth upon the throne, and unto the Lamb." (Revelation 7:9-10)

Drawing Near Activity: The Binding of Isaac was Abraham's defining moment. His story falls gently from this monumental event. But it was the triumph he had trained for since his first conversation with God. He had trained to hear and recognize God's voice to him. He had disciplined himself to obey immediately. He had schooled himself in trusting God to the point of not wavering. He had learned he could act on God's word and God would supply whatever was needed.

It wasn't an immediate transformation. It was more like a journey supported by the steps he had already taken. The important thing was God was with him in every step. God never quit or gave up on Abraham. Abraham never quit or gave up on God.

Where are you on your journey of having faith? Take the time to assess your progression. Be mindful of the mercies of God and thank Him for them. Determine not to give up. God has already provided for your success.

If you are born again, you have so much more than Abraham had. You have the Spirit who raised Jesus from the dead inside you. You have the Son of the Living God alive in your heart. Look up and see the Lamb He has provided. Your struggle is over. "Wherefore seeing we also are compassed about with so great a cloud of witnesses, let us lay aside every weight, and the sin which doth so easily beset us, and let us run with patience the race that is set before us, Looking unto Jesus the author and finisher of our faith." (Hebrews 12:1-2)

Chapter 8 General Questions

1. Why is Mt. Moriah an important place?

2. Explain Islam's story about Muhammad visiting the Temple Mount and why it couldn't have happened.

3. According to archaeology, what is the oldest mention of Jerusalem outside of the Bible?

4. What is the "Binding of Isaac?"

5. Why did God call Isaac Abraham's only son?

6. Do you think Abraham understood the concept of what we call the Triune God– Father, Son and Holy Spirit? Why or why not?

7. How is testing in the Old Testament related to obedience?

8. What is the difference between testing and temptation?

9. How old was Isaac when Abraham made the trip to Mt. Moriah?

Activity: Name the similarities between the Binding of Isaac and the events of Jesus' crucifixion.

10. How do we know Abraham believed God would raise Isaac from the dead?

11. What do you think gave Abraham the courage to be obedient to God's command to offer Isaac?

12. How do we know Isaac was willing to do what his father asked?

13. When did Jesus' followers begin to understand the meaning of the Binding of Isaac?

14. What is the significance of God providing the male sheep on Mt. Moriah?

15. Is the sculpture called Ram in a Thicket found by Leonard C. Woolley proof Abraham's story is made up? Explain your answer.

16. How does the Hebrew word *'ayil* give testimony to Jesus?

17. What is the connection between Rosh Hashanah and the Binding of Isaac?

18. What name did Abraham give Mt. Moriah and what did it mean?

19. Why do you think the Bible's statement that Abraham mourned "Sarah" is significant?

20. Describe the Cave of the Patriarchs.

21. What is the longest part of Abraham's story in Genesis?

22. Is their archaeological evidence for a servant choosing a wife? If so, explain how it applies to Abraham.

23. Who was Rebekah?

24. Who was Keturah?

25. Briefly outline Isaac's life compared to Abraham's.

Activity: List Abraham's sons and their lands. What details do we know about them?

Drawing Near Activity: What difficult thing have you been asked to do? How did you handle it?

Many times people say they want to know God's will for their lives. They may not realize knowing His will opens them to the responsibility of willfully obeying or disobeying it. Never seeking God's will for your life is one kind of wrong, but knowing and disobeying is another. Ask Jonah. Read the book of Jonah in the Old Testament if you haven't heard his story. What happened to Jonah and why?

The truth is, you will never be truly happy or fulfilled until you accept God's purpose for your life: to accept His love for you. God never intended that you do the difficult things on your own. He wants to travel with you to your Mt. Moriah because He has already provided everything you need to leave there in victory.

Chapter Evaluation

Student may write what they learned from this chapter, using a paragraph essay format. Suggested: 500 words or one page. Alternative: Student may give an oral report or Charlotte Mason style narration. Or student may complete the test provided below.

Chapter 8 Test Questions

1. Why is Mt. Moriah an important place?

2. What name did Abraham give Mt. Moriah and what did it mean?

3. What is the "Binding of Isaac?"

4. Why did God call Isaac Abraham's only son?

5. What is the difference between testing and temptation?

6. How do we know Abraham believed God would raise Isaac from the dead?

7. Who was Keturah?

8. What is the connection between Rosh Hashanah and the Binding of Isaac?

9. When did Jesus' followers begin to understand the meaning of the Binding of Isaac?

10. How does the Hebrew word *'ayil* give testimony to Jesus?

Optional essay question: Briefly outline Isaac's life compared to Abraham's. Or, Why do you think the Bible's statement that Abraham mourned "Sarah" is significant?

Chapter 9

Abraham's Legacy

Devotion

Have your Bible, a journal and pen handy. Look up the verses quoted. Read them, the verses around them, and write down what you learn.

Our life speaks. Building a legacy begins when we are young.

Abraham was chosen for a reason. The Bible tells us God is on the lookout for those He can bless. "For the eyes of the LORD run to and fro throughout the whole earth, to shew himself strong in the behalf of them whose heart is perfect toward him."(2Chronicles 16:9) Abraham apparently caught His attention. But how do you catch God's attention?

Šālēm is translated perfect in the above verse and it means complete, at peace and friendly. This implies that this person has an attitude of humble obedience toward God. Humility pleases God and opens the door to His help. "Likewise, ye younger, submit yourselves unto the elder. Yea, all of you be subject one to another, and be clothed with humility: for God resisteth the proud, and giveth grace to the humble." (1Peter 5:5) Grace is favor we do not deserve. Here we learn God gives it to the humble.

Being humble toward God enables us to embrace what God says to do. It helps us to accept correction and instruction. We say this kind of person is teachable. Another word the Bible uses for humility is meek. "The meek will he guide in judgment: and the meek will he teach his way." (Psalm 25:9) To be this type of humble will bring honor. "The fear of the LORD is the instruction of wisdom; and before honour is humility." (Proverbs 15:33)

God requires humility of His people, along with mercy and doing the right thing. "He hath shewed thee, O man, what is good; and what doth the LORD require of thee, but to do justly, and to love mercy, and to walk humbly with thy God?" (Micah 6:8) We are to love mercy. We don't offer mercy grudgingly or hesitantly. We are quick to practice it.

Obedience is a big word we don't always like to hear. Especially when we are young. It boils down to doing what you are told to do whether you want to or not. God wants this kind of obedience practiced concerning His word.

God chose Joshua as Israel's leader and gave him strict instructions. "Only be thou strong and very courageous, that thou mayest observe to do according to all the law, which Moses my servant commanded thee: turn not from it to the right hand or to the left, that thou mayest prosper whithersoever thou goest. This book of the law shall not depart out of thy mouth; but thou shalt meditate therein day and night, that thou mayest observe to do according to all that is written therein: for then thou shalt make thy way prosperous, and then thou shalt have good success." (Joshua 1:7-8)

Jesus said, "If ye love me, keep my commandments." (John 14:15) If we say we love God, but never practice what the Bible tells us to do, we are only fooling ourselves. Obedience matters to God.

So does faith. Jesus told the crowds they shouldn't give all their effort for things that are not lasting. They wanted to know what kind of work they should strive for with all their might in order to please God and to do what He did. Jesus told them to put their effort into believing Him. "Then said they unto him, What shall we do, that we might work the works of God? Jesus answered and said unto them, This is the work of God, that ye believe on him whom he hath sent." (John 6:28-29)

If Abraham has taught us anything on his journey, it is that faith requires us to be diligent and on guard against the subtleties of doubt. Jesus calls it labor, *ergazomai*. We don't labor to be saved. We *ergazomai*, toil and are engaged in believing Him.

The Bible warns that to have faith requires a fight. "Fight the good fight of faith, lay hold on eternal life, whereunto thou art also called, and hast professed a good profession before many witnesses." (1 Timothy 6:12) Having trust in God and remaining in that place is not easy, but it is the only way to please God. "But without faith it is impossible to please him: for he that cometh to God must believe that he is, and that he is a rewarder of them that diligently seek him." (Hebrews 11:6)

Humility, obedience, trust. These are qualities we see in Abraham. These are traits that grew as his relationship with God grew. Abraham was just a man. But by doing the right thing, one step after the other, he received honor and built a legacy of faith we can all be part of today.

Drawing Near Activity: How do we strengthen our trust in God? The Bible tells us that faith comes by hearing God's word (Romans 10:17). We will only have as much trust in God as we have knowledge of His word. When we act on what we know, we start strengthening our trust. We need to read the word aloud to ourselves and think on it. Memorize it and think of it throughout the day like God told Joshua.

Write on a 3x5 card whatever verses you want to memorize or speak to yourself and think on. Keep it with you so you can pull it out during the day and read the word. These are special verses you are pondering right now.

Reading the Bible should still be a priority, but the verses on your card are specific promises or principles you are "working" on. Be especially mindful of those that seem to leap off the page or attract your attention. This is the word speaking to you. Write those verses down. They are yours to teach you and to supply you for whatever your need is at the moment.

Chapter 9 General Questions

1. Read Galatians 3. In your own words, explain the concept of being Abraham's seed and heirs according to the promise.

2. What title do Christians give Abraham?

3. Why is Abraham important to the people living in the Middle East?

4. What are some misconceptions about Abraham?

5. What significant biblical character was still living when Abraham lived?

6. Discoveries at what archaeological sites have supported the Bible's account of Abraham and given us more insight?

7. If the details of Abraham's story have been backed up by archaeology, what does that suggest about the rest of his account?

8. Briefly explain what archaeology has added to our knowledge of Abraham.

9. What was Abraham's path to success?

10. What did Abraham have to receive?

11. List what Abraham has taught us about faith and briefly describe each in your own words.

Activity: Read Romans 4:18-22. Of this New Testament account of Abraham, what stands out to you right now? Make it a point of prayer to God.

12. What has Abraham taught us about covenants?

13. What do you think is the most important part of Abraham's legacy?

14. List seven things Abraham teaches us about faith.

Chapter Evaluation

Student may write what they learned from this chapter, using a paragraph essay format. Suggested: 500 words or one page. Alternative: Student may give an oral report or Charlotte Mason style narration. Or student may complete the test provided below.

Chapter 9 Test Questions

1. What does this verse mean "If we are Christ's then we are Abraham's seed and heirs according to the promise?" (Galatians 3:29)

2. List seven things Abraham teaches us about faith.

3. Discoveries at what archaeological sites have supported the Bible's account of Abraham and given us more insight?

4. Why is Abraham important to the people living in the Middle East?

5. What are some misconceptions about Abraham?

6. What significant biblical character was still living when Abraham lived?

7. Outline Abraham's path to success.

8. If the details of Abraham's story have been backed up by archaeology, what does that suggest about the rest of his account?

9. What title do Christians give Abraham?

10. What was vital that Abraham receive from God?

Optional essay question: What do you think is the most important part of Abraham's legacy? Or, What is a covenant and what has Abraham taught us about them?

Answer Keys

Chapter 1 Devotion Questions

Devotion Drawing Near Activity: Answer the questions below.

What forms your identity and determines your destiny? Why?
Answers may vary.

Why is it important to know what God says about you?
Answers may vary but should include the idea that God tells us what is available, what is possible, and what His desires for us are.

What is the place of faith?
Being fully persuaded. When you are standing by what you believe to be true and acting on it (not being afraid, praising God for deliverance, etc. are examples for the believer)despite your circumstances.

Why is knowledge and admiration of God's word not considered faith?
Knowledge means you possess the facts or the truth. Admiration means you like those facts and truths. Faith requires that you trust them enough to act on them.

How does faith come?
By hearing the anointed word of God.

How does everyone operate on faith?
Everyone acts according to what they trust or believe to be true.

What was Abraham's revelation?
Answers may vary but should include the idea that God is real, He can be trusted and His word is true.

What does it mean to choose the authority speaking into your life?
You choose who you will listen to and do what they advise you to do.

Chapter 1 General Questions

1. Are people's names important? Why or why not?
Yes; names have the power to create or define us through what we believe or what others believe about them. pgs7-8

Activity: For extra insight, read 1Chronicles 4:9-10 about Jabez. Did Jabez think his name could define him or his future? Why or why not? What does Jabez' experience tell you about God?
Jabez did think his name mattered because his name meant to grieve or to be sorrowful, and he prayed that he would not be affected by it. 1Chronicles4:10 "and that thou wouldest keep me from evil, that it may not grieve me!" Answers will vary by experience of student.

2. Explain what you learned about the term habiru.
Ancient inscriptions described them as destructive, rebellious, independent, living in tents, hired for military campaigns and from a societal aspect not an ethnic one. Amarna Tablets describe them as the Israelites invading Canaan during the time of Joshua's takeover of Canaan. But habiru are not always Israelites. It is a general word to describe a people of a certain type. pgs9-11

3. What is the biblical definition of the word Hebrew?
A descendant of Eber, one from beyond. pg 11

4. What is important about the land of the *shasu*?
The people worshipped Yahweh there. pg12

5. Why was the discovery of the Royal Archives in Ebla significant?

Its language was closely related to Hebrew. There were bilingual tablets that helped scholars translate other ancient languages. Names were found for gods, people and cities that are also in the Bible. Ancient Semitic words were discovered that matched unknown versions of words in the Bible suggesting eyewitness accounts. pgs 12-18

6. What do ancient words in the Bible suggest? (Ancient words like *mw* and *Kamāš*, for example.)
The Bible accounts were written by eyewitnesses and not inserted at a later date. pg 14

7. Compare King Ebrium of Ebla with Eber listed in Genesis 10.
Ebrium in Hebrew is Eber. King Ebrium ruled in the area near towns having the same names as Eber's descendants. The use of Ya was added to the Eblaite language during King Ebrium's reign. It is not known if Ebrium is the biblical Eber, however. pgs17-18

8. Who were the Amorites?
Distant cousins of Abraham descended from Ham who spoke a language similar to Hebrew. Mari was their capital. They were mentioned in ancient texts by various names and described in a Sumerian legend. pgs18- 23

9. Describe the ancient city of Mari.
Located on a slope west of the Euphrates River and southeast of Ebla. It had canals built to take advantage of nearby trade routes and eventually controlled trade on the river. An outer wall and an inner wall circled the city. Residents lived in mudbrick homes with indoor "plumbing". Mari had a close relationship with the Sumerian city of Ur. pg19

10. What do the Mari Texts reveal about the Bible?

People shared a common culture in the region and the Texts listed names, places and cultural practices described in the Bible. pg 20-21

Chapter 1 Test Questions

1. What do we know about the term habiru?
Ancient inscriptions used the word to describe certain people as destructive, rebellious, independent, who lived in tents, were hired for military campaigns and formed a societal group not an ethnic one. Amarna Tablets used the word to describe the Israelites invading Canaan during the time of Joshua's takeover of Canaan. But habiru are not always Israelites. It is a general word to describe a people of a certain type.

2. What is the biblical definition of the word Hebrew?
A descendant of Eber, one from beyond.

3. Why was the discovery of the Royal Archives in Ebla significant?
Its language was closely related to Hebrew. There were bilingual tablets that helped scholars translate other ancient languages. Names were found for gods, people and cities that are also in the Bible. Ancient Semitic words were discovered that matched unknown versions of words in the Bible suggesting eyewitness accounts.

4. What do ancient words in the Bible like *mw* and *Kamāš*, suggest to us about the Bible? *The Bible accounts were written by eyewitnesses and not inserted at a later date.*

5. Who was King Ebrium?
King Ebrium was an Eblaite king who ruled in the area near towns having the same names as Eber's descendants. The use of Ya was added to the Eblaite language during King Ebrium's reign. While some scholars think he is Abraham's ancestor Eber, it is not known if Ebrium is the biblical Eber.

6. What biblical character do some scholars think King Ebrium may be?
Eber.

7. Describe the Amorites.
Distant cousins of Abraham descended from Ham who spoke a language similar to Hebrew. Mari was their capital. They were mentioned in ancient texts by various names and described in a Sumerian legend. They had similar characteristics as Hebrews.

8. What are some things we know about the ancient city of Mari?
It was located on a slope west of the Euphrates River and southeast of Ebla. It had canals built to take advantage of nearby trade routes and eventually controlled trade on the river. An outer wall and an inner wall circled the city. Residents lived in mudbrick homes with indoor "plumbing". Mari had a close relationship with the Sumerian city of Ur.

9. What do the Mari Texts reveal about the Bible?
People shared a common culture in the region and the Texts listed names, places and cultural practices described in the Bible.

10. Was Abraham an Amorite? Why or why not?
The Bible says he was a descendent of Eber.

Optional essay question: Why are names important? Give examples.
Answer should include the concept of how words we hear and what we believe about them influence what we believe to be possible. Abraham or Jabez may be an example or any of the student's choice.

Answer Keys 117

Chapter 2 General Questions

1. Describe the three Urs scholars consider may be linked to Abraham. *Answer may include any of the information from pages 27-37.*

Urkesh *is called Tell Mozan today in northeast Syria, 400 miles from Damascus, also near Göbekli Tepe, Serug and Nahor, Chagar Bazar, Tell Brak. The 300 acre city was bigger than Ebla. Located almost a hundred miles slightly north and east of Harran, it was an important trade city lying on the east west route.*

Urfa *is west of Urkesh and six miles from Göbekli Tepe. Some scholars believe this Ur to be Abraham's hometown. These northern cities, Urkesh and Urfa included, dated to the time of Abraham and were connected by trade and politics. Urfa is called Sanliurfa today.*

Urim, Ur, Iraq. *Claimed to be Abraham's Ur by C. Leonard Woolley. Ur was a major port city of the Persian Gulf, situated on the west bank near the mouth of the Euphrates in the Third Millennium BC. Today it is called Tell el-Muqayyar.*

2. Name some important archaeological finds relating to each Ur. *Answer may include any of the information from pages 27-37.*

Urkesh *was a Hurrian city dating to the time of Ebla. Residents spoke Hurrian which is not related to Hebrew but is an Indo-European or Sumerian language. City was 300 acres. Hurrians were more advanced than first believed, having plumbing and architecture to rival other sites in Mesopotamia. Excavated by Georgio Buccellati and Marilyn Kelly-Buccellati.*

Urfa *had a huge religious center dedicated to pagan gods. Urfa was a trading center, and later conquered by all the major empires, including Sumer, Ebla, Babylon and Akkad.*

At Ur, *people studied astronomy and gave us number systems based on one, ten and six. They had a writing method we call Sumerian cuneiform. At Ur, ancient royal tombs, organized neighborhoods, musical instruments, literature, poems, schools and libraries revealed a rich culture. Ur was a merchant city with the latest news, goods and designs of Mesopotamia pouring into and out of its boundaries. Farmers brought in livestock and crops for rituals and sacrifices, for wool, hides and food. Gold came from as far away as Aratta (Armenia), Turkey, Iran and Dilmun. Wood came from Canaan or India. Ur's merchants traded with people from the Indus civilization over a thousand miles away for rust colored gems called carnelian. These gems were carved into beads. The merchants traveled to modern day Afghanistan to get the rich blue lapis lazuli rock and polished stones which were used to make jewelry, idols, government seals and other decorations. Copper came from Oman. Chlorite, a mineral, came from Iran and was used by craftsmen to carve seals, beads and to form goblets and containers ranging in color from dark green to light gray. Some vessels were dedicated to Sumerian gods. Towering over the city was the ziggurat built by Ur-Nammu for Nanna, the moon god. Golden bulls were found on lyres and charms. Houses were unearthed that had stairs leading to the roof and had rooms built off a central courtyard. They resemble the modern homes of families in Iraq today.*

3. What is Agatha Christie's connection to the Sumerian city of Ur?
She was married to Woolley's assistant Max Mallowan.pg 36

4. Describe the biblical Ur.
The Bible states Abraham's father lived in 'ûr of the kaśdîy, Ur of the Chaldees. pg 37

5. Describe what the Bible has to say about the Chaldeans or the *Kasdîy*.
The word translated Chaldees is Kasdîy (kass DEEN). It refers to an astrologer or a descendant of Kesed, a Kasdite. Kesed is listed as one of Nahor's sons in Genesis 22:22. He is Abraham's nephew. Kasdîy can even mean toward the Kasdites. pg 37-38

6. What is the name of Abraham's homeland according to the Bible and in what modern countries is this region located today?
Ăram Nahărayim, modern Syria and Turkey. pg 40

7. Why are the Nuzi Tablets important to the Genesis accounts?
Nuzi was an ancient city connected to other ancient cities—like Urkesh—during the time of the patriarchs, recording the life of the ancient world's ordinary, average citizen in legal documents. The Nuzi Tablets support the traditions written by the patriarchs concerning slaves inheriting property (Genesis 15:2), possessing household gods as proof of a legal right to an estate (Genesis 31:19), children through a concubine (Genesis 16:2-3), blessings pronounced over children from dying parents (Genesis 27:4), selling a birthright (Genesis 25:29-34) and family records being kept. pg 32-33

8. Why were cities safer than the open country?
Cities were walled to protect its residents from outsiders and cities had armies. pg 41

9. What pagan gods were worshipped in Ur?
False gods like gold bulls, elaborately engraved statues of man-like gods, Humbaba, the guardian of the Cedar Forests, Sin, Nanna and Scorpion Man. pg 29, 41

10. Who was Henry Rawlinson?
Henry Rawlinson was a man who learned to read the scratchings on tablets called cuneiform. In 1849, he read an inscription on a brick brought back to England by another archaeologist. His translation surprised everyone because it said Ur. pg 35

11. Who was Iscah and what does Jewish tradition say concerning her?
Iscah was one of Haran's daughters. She was Abraham's niece. Jewish tradition says Iscah was another name for Sarai. pg 43

12. Describe what we know about Abraham's family according to the Bible.
They lived north of the Euphrates in Ăram Nahărayim which is modern Syria and Turkey, and they worshipped idols. pg 33, 34, 40

13. Why might Terah have decided to move to Canaan?
Some reasons scholars consider are: Abraham may have told him what God said to him, Terah may have felt called to go to Canaan, his son Haran died, there may have been war. pg 41-44

14. Why might Terah have "stopped" in Harran?
He may have gotten sick or weak. He may have wanted to live and trade there. He may have wanted to worship there. pg 41-44

15. Define *yâshab*.
To sit down. pg 44

Chapter 2 Test Questions

1. Give a brief description of each Ur.
Answer may include any of the information from pages 27-37.

Urkesh *is called Tell Mozan today in northeast Syria, 400 miles from Damascus, also near Göbekli Tepe, Serug and Nahor, Chagar Bazar, Tell Brak. The 300 acre city was bigger than Ebla. Located almost a hundred miles slightly north and east of Harran, it was an important trade city lying on the east west route.*

Urfa *is west of Urkesh and six miles from Göbekli Tepe. Some scholars believe this Ur to be Abraham's hometown. These northern cities, Urkesh and Urfa included, dated to the time of Abraham and were connected by trade and politics. Urfa is called Sanliurfa today.*

Urim, Ur, Iraq. *Claimed to be Abraham's Ur by C. Leonard Woolley. Ur was a major port city of the Persian Gulf, situated on the west bank near the mouth of the Euphrates in the Third Millennium BC. Today it is called Tell el-Muqayyar.*

2. Name some important archaeological finds relating to each Ur.
Answer may include any of the information from pages 27-37.

Urkesh *was a Hurrian city dating to the time of Ebla. Residents spoke Hurrian which is not related to Hebrew but is an Indo-European or Sumerian language. City was 300 acres. Hurrians were more advanced than first believed, having plumbing and architecture to rival other sites in Mesopotamia. Excavated by Georgio Buccellati and Marilyn Kelly-Buccellati.*
Urfa *had a huge religious center dedicated to pagan gods. Urfa was a trad-*

ing center, and later conquered by all the major empires, including Sumer, Ebla, Babylon and Akkad.

At Ur, people studied astronomy and gave us number systems based on one, ten and six. They had a writing method we call Sumerian cuneiform. At Ur, ancient royal tombs, organized neighborhoods, musical instruments, literature, poems, schools and libraries revealed a rich culture. Ur was a merchant city with the latest news, goods and designs of Mesopotamia pouring into and out of its boundaries. Farmers brought in livestock and crops for rituals and sacrifices, for wool, hides and food. Gold came from as far away as Aratta (Armenia), Turkey, Iran and Dilmun. Wood came from Canaan or India. Ur's merchants traded with people from the Indus civilization over a thousand miles away for rust colored gems called carnelian. These gems were carved into beads. The merchants traveled to modern day Afghanistan to get the rich blue lapis lazuli rock and polished stones which were used to make jewelry, idols, government seals and other decorations. Copper came from Oman. Chlorite, a mineral, came from Iran and was used by craftsmen to carve seals, beads and to form goblets and containers ranging in color from dark green to light gray. Some vessels were dedicated to Sumerian gods. Towering over the city was the ziggurat built by Ur-Nammu for Nanna, the moon god. Golden bulls were found on lyres and charms. Houses were unearthed that had stairs leading to the roof and had rooms built off a central courtyard. They resemble the modern homes of families in Iraq today.

3. What is the name and location of Abraham's homeland?
Ăram Nahărayim, modern Syria and Turkey.

4. What is Agatha Christie's connection to the Sumerian city of Ur?
She was married to Woolley's assistant Max Mallowan.

5. What does the Bible say about the Chaldeans or the *Kasdîy*?
The word translated Chaldees is Kasdîy (kass DEEN). It refers to an astrologer or a descendant of Kesed, a Kasdite. Kesed is listed as one of Nahor's sons in Genesis 22:22. He is Abraham's nephew. Kasdîy can even mean toward the Kasdites.

6. According to the Bible, what do we know about Abraham's family?
They lived north of the Euphrates in Ăram Nahărayim which is modern Syria and Turkey, and they worshipped idols.

7. Why are the Nuzi Tablets important to the Genesis accounts?
Nuzi was an ancient city connected to other ancient cities—like Urkesh—during the time of the patriarchs, recording the life of the ancient world's ordinary, average citizen in legal documents. The Nuzi Tablets support the traditions written by the patriarchs concerning slaves inheriting property (Genesis 15:2), possessing household gods as proof of a legal right to an estate (Genesis 31:19), children through a concubine (Genesis 16:2-3), blessings pronounced over children from dying parents (Genesis 27:4), selling a birthright (Genesis 25:29-34) and family records being kept.

8. Why were cities safer than the open country?
Cities were walled to protect its residents from outsiders and cities had armies.

9. What was the name of the city where Abraham stopped after leaving Ur?   *Harran*

10. Define *yâshab*.
To sit down.

Optional essay question: Which Ur may have the strongest biblical and archaeological evidence to be Abraham's Ur? Support your answer with scriptures and archaeological data.
Answers will vary to first question according to student's perspective, but a defense of their choice is required.

Chapter 3 General Questions

1. Describe the city of Harran.
Harran was situated on a flat plain, northeast of the Euphrates near the Balikh River. An archaeological site at Tell Sabi Abyad has shown that pottery was produced there for the trade market. Clay tokens, used for exchange, date to 5,000 BC by an evolutionary timeline. Cattle, pigs, sheep and goats were raised along with einkorn wheat, barley, flax, lentils and peas. The area continued to be inhabited throughout the time of the major empires. Its location near the Balikh gave it its importance. Harran lay about six hundred miles north, by river, from Ur, Iraq. Like a shimmering, liquid ribbon, the Euphrates connected the trade cities and both were major centers of worship for Sin. pg 49

2. Where does Abraham's life story fit in our dates for history?
Early Bronze Age 1. pg 51-53

3. What belief or theory complicates dating biblical history?
Evolution. pg 52-53

4. What is the biblical total of years for man's history so far?
Six thousand. pg 52

Activity: Research the evidence for a young earth. Which of the discoveries do you find most compelling?
Answers will vary.

5. What significant event happened at Hamoukar?
A war over a tool factory. pg 54

6. What are some reasons scholars give for why Terah might have wanted to move to Canaan?
Terah was a merchant or an idol maker and wanted to establish his business there. The area suffered a period of war and decline referred to as a Dark Age. There was a famine. pg 50-55

7. Explain slavery in the Early Bronze Age.
Slavery in ancient times was not always a matter of one person owning another. It could be a contract between two people on a work agreement. The tenure could be short or it could be for life. This type of slave was protected by laws and had rights. This wasn't a slavery based on skin color; it happened to people who lost their freedom because they were kidnapped or conquered in war, or not able to pay off debt to a debt collector. Some people sold themselves into slavery. Some sold their children. During a famine, a child could be sold into slavery so it could be fed. Criminals could be made slaves as punishment. Foreigners were especially targeted for involuntary slavery. Harsh treatment was a reality for many slaves who could not pay the contracted redemption price. If they couldn't pay, the slave fell lower in status, like a criminal slave. These slaves were marked with tattoos, like on a shaven head for example. Some wore a special pierced ear tag. This piercing differed from the common pierced ears of women and men during the time period. These slaves could be legally mistreated within certain guidelines. We call this group chattel slaves. But debt slaves or other slaves were treated as employees, and debt slavery was limited to a number of years. Slaves could potentially marry another slave or a free person, own property, conduct business and buy their freedom. pg 56-57

Activity: Using the maps at the end of chapters 1 &2, plot the routes Abraham may have taken from Harran into Canaan.

From Harran south to Damascus and used the trade routes south from there into the eastern regions of Canaan and turning onto the route going to Shechem or, straight south following a route (The King's Highway) east of the Jordan and entering Canaan through the pass near Mt. Ebal.

8. Define Moreh.
Moreh in Hebrew can mean teacher or early rain, and its root word means one who shoots an arrow. pg 59

9. Why is Moreh an important site?
It was the belly or the middle of the land. The tree growing there was a landmark, and it became a landmark of faith for the Israelites. pg 59-61

10. What city was later built near Moreh?
Shechem. pg 59

11. What are two events that happened in Shechem that link the Old Testament to the New Testament?
It became a place of Israel's deceit and a witness to their unfaithfulness. Jesus came and sat with a wayward, despised Samaritan, an image of unfaithfulness. But to this woman, in that place He openly proclaimed Himself as the Messiah. pg 61

12. What does Bethel mean?
House of God. pg 62

13. What did Abraham begin to do between the cities of Bethel and Ai?
Call upon the Lord. pg 62

14. Describe what Abraham's tents and camp may have looked like.
They may have been black and made out of goat hair. The tents may have been large, with black roofs and separate, lighter colored side pieces. The side pieces could have been raised to let in the breeze or lowered for privacy and shelter. The tents may have been arranged in a sprawling circle. pg 62-63

15. How did Abraham think of himself?
As a foreigner or sojourner. pg 63

16. What did a Syrian farmer discover by accident?
The farmer found the city of Ugarit. pg 64

17. Did the Canaanite tablets found at Ras Shamra, Syria, confirm what the Bible said about Canaanite culture?
Yes. pg 65-66

18. What two religions are connected to Abraham?
Judaism and Christianity. pg 66-67

19. What problem did Abraham face soon after entering Canaan?
A severe famine began. pg 67

20. How could the ancient Middle East have supported the large flocks and herds represented in the Bible?
Archaeology has shown the climate was wetter in the Early Bronze Age than it is today. pg 67

21. What did Abraham decide to do to solve the problem he faced after arriving in Canaan?
Go to Egypt because the famine was severe. pg 67-68

22. What did Abraham think his next problem was going to be in going to Egypt?
Men would see Sarah's beauty and want to have her as their wife. They would kill him so they could marry her. pg 68-69

23. What was his solution?
They should say Sarah was his sister not his wife. pg 68

24. What happened to Sarah because of Abraham's solution?
She was taken by Pharaoh to be one of his wives. pg70

Chapter 3 Test Questions

1. Where does Abraham's life story fit in our dates for history?
Early Bronze Age 1.

2. Why is Moreh an important site?
It was the belly or the middle of the land. The tree growing there was a landmark, and it became a landmark of faith for the Israelites.

3. What is the biblical total of years for man's history so far?
Six thousand.

4. What was slavery like in the Early Bronze Age?
Slavery in ancient times was not always a matter of one person owning another. It could be a contract between two people on a work agreement. The tenure could be short or it could be for life. This type of slave was protected by laws and had rights. This wasn't a slavery based on skin color; it happened to people who lost their freedom because they were kidnapped or conquered in war, or not able to pay off debt to a debt collector. Some people sold themselves into slavery. Some sold their children. During a famine, a child could be sold into slavery so it could be fed. Criminals could be made slaves as punishment. Foreigners were especially targeted for involuntary slavery. Harsh treatment was a reality for many slaves who could not pay the contracted redemption price. If they couldn't pay, the slave fell lower in status, like a criminal slave. These slaves were marked with tattoos, like on a shaven head for example. Some wore a special pierced ear tag. This piercing differed from the common pierced ears of women and men during the time period. These slaves could be legally mistreated within certain guidelines. We call this group chattel slaves. But debt slaves or other slaves were treated as employees, and debt slavery was limited to a number of years.

Slaves could potentially marry another slave or a free person, own property, conduct business and buy their freedom.

5. Did the Canaanite tablets found at Ras Shamra, Syria, confirm what the Bible said about Canaanite culture? Why or why not?
Yes, there was idolatry, perverse practices, child sacrifices and general lawlessness.

6. What two religions are connected to Abraham?
Judaism and Christianity.

7. What problem did Abraham face soon after entering Canaan?
Famine.

8. How could the ancient Middle East have supported the large flocks and herds represented in the Bible?
The ancient climate was wetter.

9. What did Abraham decide to do to solve the problem he faced after arriving in Canaan?
Go to Egypt.

10. What did Abraham think his next problem was going to be in going to Egypt?
He would be in danger because Sarah was beautiful.

Optional essay question: Compare the city of Harran with the land of Canaan. *Answers should include the common cultural practices, the idolatry* shared *and the rural culture of Canaan.*

Chapter 4 General Questions

1. Do you think Abraham made a mistake when he went to Egypt? Why or Why not?
Answers may vary.

2. What do you think might have been the hardest part of the situation in Egypt for Sarah to deal with? Explain your answer.
Answers will vary.

3. The incident that involved Sarah, Abraham and Pharaoh in Egypt foreshadows what later event in Israel's history?
Israel's captivity in Egypt, the plagues and the Exodus. pg 78

4. Why does the Bible say Abraham and Sarah "went up" out of Egypt?
The land rises. pg 78

5. Describe the Negev.
Answer may include any of the information from pages 78-79 such as craggy peaks, desert, wild animals like leopards, lions, antelope, etc., closed valleys called makhteshim, dangerous floods, hot temperatures, plains.

6. What is the controversy over Abraham's camels?
Some scholars don't believe he had camels because camels were not domesticated at the time of Abraham. pg 79- 80

7. How is the controversy solved?
Archaeology has discovered many evidences of one humped camels in the region of Egypt and two humped camels in the northern regions beyond

Syria and in the regions nearby, all of which date to the time of Abraham and before. pg 80-83

8. To what Canaanite cities did Abraham return to after he left Egypt?
Bethel and Ai. pg 85

9. Explain who the Canaanites were.
They were a mix of tribes ranging from northern Syria, south to the border of Egypt and east of the Jordan River. Arkites, Arvadite, Sinite, Zemarkites, Amorites, Hamathites, Girgashites, Hivites, Jebusites, Hethites, Perizzite. pg 85-88

10. Write God's covenant with Abraham in your own words.
Answers will vary but should include the blessings offered to Abraham and his descendents and to his "Seed."

11. What is the importance of God's promises to Abraham and are they valid today?
God promised to bless Abraham. He promised that those who blessed Abraham would be blessed. Those who cursed him would be cursed. This extended to Abraham's descendents. God promised to bless Abraham's seed. Abrahm's "seed" referred to Jesus, and if we are "in" Jesus then we too are Abraham's seed and recipients of all his promises because God never ended His covenant with Abraham. pg 88-90

12. Describe the situation with Lot.
Lot's herdsman started arguing with Abraham's herdsmen. The cattle were mixing, trespassing. The livestock was hungry and thirsty. It got crowded and stressful. They separated and Lot went east. pg 91

13. What are your thoughts concerning Lot's choice?
Answers will vary.

14. How did Abraham's kindness to Lot prove his trust in God?
He believed God would uphold His agreement to bless him wherever he went in Canaan so he gave Lot first choice of the land. pg 91

15. In what way(s) did God encourage Abraham?
God was going to give him all the land of Canaan and make his descendents like the dust of the earth, meaning there were so many they couldn't be counted. pg 92

Chapter 4 Test Questions

1. What happened to Sarah and Abraham in Egypt?
Sarah was taken by Pharaoh's men and Abraham was given gifts. Then they were given an escort out of Egypt after Pharaoh's household was stricken with a plague. God showed them mercy and delivered them.

2. The incident that involved Sarah, Abraham and Pharaoh in Egypt foreshadows what later event in Israel's history?
Israel's captivity in Egypt, the plagues and the Exodus.

3. Why does the Bible say Abraham and Sarah "went up" out of Egypt?
The land rises.

4. Describe the Negev.
Answer may include any of the information from pages 78-79
May include craggy peaks, desert, wild animals like leopards, lions, antelope, etc., closed valleys called makhteshim, dangerous floods, hot temperatures, plains.

5. What is the controversy over Abraham's camels?
Some scholars don't believe he had camels because camels were not domesticated at the time of Abraham.

6. How is the controversy solved?
Archaeology has discovered many evidences of one humped camels in the region of Egypt and two humped camels in the northern regions beyond Syria and in the regions nearby, all of which date to the time of Abraham and before.

Answer Keys

7. Who were the Canaanites and what were they like?
They were the inhabitants of Canaan who practiced idolatry, immorality and lawlessness. They were a mix of tribes ranging from northern Syria, south to the border of Egypt and east of the Jordan River. Arkites, Arvadite, Sinite, Zemarkites, Amorites, Hamathites, Girgashites, Hivites, Jebusites, Hethites, Perizzite.

8. What was included in God's covenant with Abraham?
Answers will vary but should include the blessings offered to Abraham and his descendents and to his "Seed."

9. Who was Lot and what was the situation between him and Abraham?
Lot was Abraham's nephew. Lot's herdsman started arguing with Abraham's herdsmen. The cattle were mixing, trespassing. The livestock was hungry and thirsty. It got crowded and stressful. They separated and Lot went east.

10. How did Abraham's kindness to Lot prove his trust in God?
He believed God would uphold His agreement to bless him wherever he went in Canaan so he gave Lot first choice of the land.

Optional essay question: What is the importance of God's promises to Abraham and are they valid today?
Answer should include elements of the following: God promised to bless Abraham. He promised that those who blessed Abraham would be blessed. Those who cursed him would be cursed. This extended to Abraham's descendents. God promised to bless Abraham's seed. Abraham's "seed" referred to Jesus, and if we are "in" Jesus then we too are Abraham's seed and recipients of all his promises because God never ended His covenant with Abraham.

Chapter 5 General Questions

1. Explain what we know about the city of Bethel.

Bethel was located in the biblical heartland of Israel. It is the second most mentioned city in the Bible after Jerusalem. Today the site of ancient Bethel is El Bireh in the West Bank. Beth-El was the place where God spoke to His people. Its original name had been Luz, but Jacob renamed it Beth-El, House of God, because there he saw angels going back and forth from heaven to earth. Joshua had brought the Israelites back to this region before he died, and people continued to return to seek God there during the time of the Judges. The Ark of the Covenant was kept in Bethel for a while. Deborah judged there, and Samuel visited there as part of his ministry to Israel. But Bethel's prestige as God's house came to an end under Jeroboam. He had a golden calf made and set it up in Bethel for the Israelites of the Northern Kingdom. pg 95-96

2. Describe Hebron and why it is an important place for Israelis and Christians.

Answer may include any of the following: Hebron means association. The ancient city was not sitting at the site of our modern Hebron. Modern Hebron spreads below Abraham's, surrounding the Cave of the Patriarchs. Abraham's Hebron is Tel Hebron near Jebel Rumeida. It has a spring, and olive trees and a type of wild mustard grow there. In Abraham's day Hebron was the most important city in the Judean hills, and it still is. Kirjatharba is another name for Hebron and so is Mamre,. Some scholars believe the city was large enough to be divided into sections or quarters. Early Bronze Age Hebron had been fortified with a wall, twenty feet thick. Large irregular rocks piled fourteen feet high, leveled with mud brick, may have originally stood over twenty feet high. There are several Hebrew tombs in Hebron: Othniel Ben Kenaz, Ruth, Jesse, Abner, and the Cave of the Patri-

archs (Abraham, Sarah, Isaac, Rebekah, Jacob and Leah). 4,000 year old stairs were discovered which led up to the city gates. Also found– an Israeli four-room house and pottery inscribed with the Hebrew word Hevron on them. Other finds included seals dating to Hezekiah on jars used for the army fighting Sennacherib perhaps, and black stains on pillars which show fire damage, probably when Sennacherib attacked the city. Abraham lived there and it was the only place where Abraham bought ground. David chose Hebron for his first capital.
It is important to Jews and Christians because of the tombs there. pg 96-98

3. What were the names of Abraham's friends living near Hebron?
Mamre, Eshcol and Aner. pg 98

4. Who was Chedorlaomer and why did he want to go to Canaan?
Chedorlaomer ruled over at least five cities in Canaan. He made them pay a tax to him. The cities paid the tax for twelve years and in the thirteenth year they rebelled. In the fourteenth, Chedorlaomer gathered three kings, vassals or allies, and came from what is today Iran to fight the rebellious kings in Canaan. pg 99

5. What is the controversy over the kings in Genesis 14?
Some think there are no kings of the Middle Bronze Period named anything close to Chedorlaomer, nothing is known about the other kings so it is decided they did not exist and many claim, since there is no evidence, the account is made up. Others are convinced, even if the kings prove at some point to be real historical figures, the Bible writers inserted the story into Genesis when they were captives in Babylon to make Abraham look important. pg 99, 107

6. Who is T.G. Pinches and why is he important to our study of Genesis 14?

Theophilus Goldridge (T.G.)Pinches was a British man who became an Assyriologist with the British Museum in 1878. Pinches came to the British Museum two years after George Smith, the man who translated the Epic of Gilgamesh, had died. Pinches is famous for correcting the spelling and pronunciation of Gilgamesh's name. He is also known for translating two Babylonian texts containing the names Tudhula, Eri-Ekua and Kudur-lachgumal, the kings from Genesis 14. pg 101-103

7. Read Genesis 14 for yourself. Name the four kings allied with Chedorlaomer, and then list the five kings from the cities on the plain.

Amraphel king of Shinar, Arioch king of Ellasar, Chedorlaomer king of Elam, and Tidal king of nations; Bera king of Sodom, Birsha king of Gomorrah, Shinab king of Admah, Shemeber king of Zeboiim, king of Bela (Zoar). Genesis 14:1-2

8. Briefly describe Chedorlaomer's campaign and the fate of the people living in or near the cities on the plain.

The first city t attacked was Ashteroth Karnaim, then the Zuzims proceeding southward to attack Shaveh Kiriathaim. Traveling south, they attacked the Horite people living near Mt.Seir and all the way to the Desert of Paran near western Saudi Arabia. Then the kings turned to attack Kadesh and back to En Gedi. The result was a clean sweep of victories in lands belonging to the Rephaim, the Amalakites and Amorites. News was carried to the five kings living east of En Gedi in Zoar, Zeboiim, Admah, Gomorrah and Sodom. The message was urgent: Chedorlaomer had circled back and was heading for the road close by; expect an attack. The five kings rallied and joined forces in hopes of defeating Chedorlaomer's allied forces.

But they had to retreat and many fell into the slime pits uncovered by the receding Dead Sea. Survivors escaped to the mountains. Chedorlaomer and his troops sacked the cities and carried off all the people and plunder they could manage. pg 108-109

9. Explain the geography of the land around the Dead Sea.
The Dead Sea during wet periods flooded the southern basin. In dry periods it receded, revealing slime pits. Today the Dead Sea is shrinking and there are even sinkholes almost seven miles deep. pg 109

10. Who is David Ben-Gad Cohen and what is important to Bible believing Christians about his research?
Dr. David Ben-Gad HaCohen is a Torah scholar who has studied the periods in history and geology to determine the approximate date this battle might have happened. Dr. HaCohen's research states the valley was flooded during the Third Millennium, causing the cities to be built on the south eastern shore. He found that by the late Third Millennium, the Early Bronze age, it was dry. It was also during this period that the cities were destroyed and never occupied again which agrees with the biblical date and its account. pg 109

11. How do the excavations at En Gedi and Dr. Osgood's research relate to Genesis 14?
At En Gedi another discovery in 1960 revealed a cave. Apparently the ancient residents of En Gedi had quickly stashed valuable articles in the cave, but no one came back to get them. It is called the Cave of Treasures. These settlements disappeared at the same time but no one knows why. Dr. Osgood states "if you plot those sites on a map and realize they all disappeared at the same time, knowing also of the urgency at En Gedi" the only thing

in history that might accommodate their disappearance is Chedorlaomer's march over the same territory. pg 109-112

12. How did Abraham find out Lot had been taken captive?
A survivor that fled told him. pg 112

13. What did Abraham do in response to the news?
He gathered 318 of the men servants born into his household along with Mamre, Eshcol and Aner and pursued Chedorlaomer and his allies, catching up to them near Dan in northern Israel. Abraham separated his troops and conducted a surprise attack, pursuing Chedolaomer and his kings as far as Damascus. Abraham won back all the captives and the goods stolen. pg 112-113

For further study:
Look at the map at the end of Chapter 1. Do you think it was possible for Elamite kings to have ruled in Sumerian cities?
Sometimes we think of ancient people in segregated bubbles, this empire or culture then that one with no overlap as if boundaries were walls. This was not true in many places on the earth and certainly not in Mesopotamia. Name five facts, biblical or archaeological, that prove this concerning our study of Abraham.
Answers will vary but should include any of the shared cultural or religious practices.

14. Why is the word *chânîyk* important?
What is important is chânîyk is used once in the Bible. But it was found in Egyptian Execration Texts dated to the Twelfth Dynasty. This points to a writer living in that era—Moses—and not a writer living when the Isra-

elites were living in Babylon hundreds of years later. pg 113

15. Who was Melchizedek?

He was the king of Salem (Jerusalem) and and High Priest of God. He refreshed Abraham's men with food and drink, and Abraham gave him an offering from the plunder they brought back. pg 113-114

16. What might archaeologist Eli Shukron have discovered in Jerusalem?

Melchizedek's altar. pg 114

17. Why do you think Abraham would not accept gifts or payment from the ruler of Sodom?

Answers will vary.

18. What was the spiritual importance of Abraham defending the people of Canaan?

He acted like the leader of the land. pg 115

19. What insight does King Suppiluliuma give us?

He provides the example of a greater king helping a lesser king(a vassal) as his responsibility and not requiring payment. pg 116

20. Do you believe there is enough biblical and archaeological evidence to solve the controversies of Genesis 14? Why or why not?

Answers may vary but should include references to support the conclusion.

Chapter 5 Test Questions

1. Describe Hebron and why it is an important place for Israelis and Christians.

Answer may include any of the following: Hebron means association. The ancient city was not sitting at the site of our modern Hebron. Modern Hebron spreads below Abraham's, surrounding the Cave of the Patriarchs. Abraham's Hebron is Tel Hebron near Jebel Rumeida. It has a spring, and olive trees and a type of wild mustard grow there. In Abraham's day Hebron was the most important city in the Judean hills, and it still is. Kirjatharba is another name for Hebron and so is Mamre,. Some scholars believe the city was large enough to be divided into sections or quarters. Early Bronze Age Hebron had been fortified with a wall, twenty feet thick. Large irregular rocks piled fourteen feet high, leveled with mud brick, may have originally stood over twenty feet high. There are several Hebrew tombs in Hebron: Othniel Ben Kenaz, Ruth, Jesse, Abner, and the Cave of the Patriarchs (Abraham, Sarah, Isaac, Rebekah, Jacob and Leah). 4,000 year old stairs were discovered which led up to the city gates. Also found— an Israeli four-room house and pottery inscribed with the Hebrew word Hevron on them. Other finds included seals dating to Hezekiah on jars used for the army fighting Sennacherib perhaps, and black stains on pillars which show fire damage, probably when Sennacherib attacked the city. Abraham lived there and it was the only place where Abraham bought ground. David chose Hebron for his first capital.

It is important to Jews and Christians because of the tombs there.

2. What was the spiritual importance of Abraham defending the people of Canaan?

He acted like the leader of the land.

3. What does Eli Shukron think he has discovered in Jerusalem?
Melchizedek's altar.

4. Who was Melchizedek?
He was the king of Salem (Jerusalem) and and High Priest of God. He refreshed Abraham's men with food and drink, and Abraham gave him an offering from the plunder they brought back.

5. Who was Chedorlaomer and why did he want to go to Canaan?
Chedorlaomer ruled over at least five cities in Canaan. He made them pay a tax to him. The cities paid the tax for twelve years and in the thirteenth year they rebelled. In the fourteenth, Chedorlaomer gathered three kings, vassals or allies, and came from what is today Iran to fight the rebellious kings in Canaan.

6. What is the controversy over the kings in Genesis 14?
Some think there are no kings of the Middle Bronze Period named anything close to Chedorlaomer, nothing is known about the other kings so it is decided they did not exist and many claim, since there is no evidence, the account is made up. Others are convinced, even if the kings prove at some point to be real historical figures, the Bible writers inserted the story into Genesis when they were captives in Babylon to make Abraham look important.

7. Who is T.G. Pinches and why is he important to our study of Genesis 14?
Theophilus Goldridge (T.G.)Pinches was a British man who became an Assyriologist with the British Museum in 1878. Pinches came to the British Museum two years after George Smith, the man who translated the Epic

of Gilgamesh, had died. Pinches is famous for correcting the spelling and pronunciation of Gilgamesh's name. He is also known for translating two Babylonian texts containing the names Tudhula, Eri-Ekua and Kudur-lachgumal, the kings from Genesis 14.

8. Who is David Ben-Gad Cohen and what is important to Bible believing Christians about his research?
Dr. David Ben-Gad HaCohen is a Torah scholar who has studied the periods in history and geology to determine the approximate date this battle might have happened. Dr. HaCohen's research states the valley was flooded during the Third Millennium, causing the cities to be built on the south eastern shore. He found that by the late Third Millennium, the Early Bronze age, it was dry. It was also during this period that the cities were destroyed and never occupied again which agrees with the biblical date and its account.

9. Why is the word *chânîyk* important?
What is important is chânîyk is used once in the Bible. But it was found in Egyptian Execration Texts dated to the Twelfth Dynasty. This points to a writer living in that era—Moses—and not a writer living when the Israelites were living in Babylon hundreds of years later.

10. How do the excavations at En Gedi and Dr. Osgood's research relate to Genesis 14?
At En Gedi another discovery in 1960 revealed a cave. Apparently the ancient residents of En Gedi had quickly stashed valuable articles in the cave, but no one came back to get them. It is called the Cave of Treasures. These settlements disappeared at the same time but no one knows why. Dr. Osgood states "if you plot those sites on a map and realize they all disappeared

at the same time, knowing also of the urgency at En Gedi" the only thing in history that might accommodate their disappearance is Chedorlaomer's march over the same territory.

Optional essay question

Briefly describe Chedorlaomer's campaign, its effect concerning the people living in or near the cities on the plain and Abraham's response.

The first city t attacked was Ashteroth Karnaim, then the Zuzims proceeding southward to attack Shaveh Kiriathaim. Traveling south, they attacked the Horite people living near Mt.Seir and all the way to the Desert of Paran near western Saudi Arabia. Then the kings turned to attack Kadesh and back to En Gedi. The result was a clean sweep of victories in lands belonging to the Rephaim, the Amalakites and Amorites. News was carried to the five kings living east of En Gedi in Zoar, Zeboiim, Admah, Gomorrah and Sodom. The message was urgent: Chedorlaomer had circled back and was heading for the road close by; expect an attack. The five kings rallied and joined forces in hopes of defeating Chedorlaomer's allied forces. But they had to retreat and many fell into the slime pits uncovered by the receding Dead Sea. Survivors escaped to the mountains. Chedorlaomer and his troops sacked the cities and carried off all the people and plunder they could manage. Abraham gathered 318 of the men servants born into his household along with Mamre, Eshcol and Aner and pursued Chedorlaomer and his allies, catching up to them near Dan in northern Israel. Abraham separated his troops and conducted a surprise attack, pursuing Chedolaomer and his kings as far as Damascus. Abraham won back all the captives and the goods stolen.

Chapter 6 General Questions

1. What bothered Abraham?

He wanted God to give him a son. pg121

2. How did God encourage him?

God told Abraham that He was his shield and exceeding great reward. Then God promised to give him a son and so many descendents he couldn't count them. pg 120, 126-127

3. Did Abraham understand God's encouragement? Explain your answer.

Abraham may not have understood at first since he wasn't comforted by God's words of assurance. He didn't grasp the meaning in God's words to him about being his source of supply. It included having a son. Abraham didn't need to fear failure because God was his shield, enabling him to be triumphant against any type of defeat. He asked about his son, and after God's answer he knew God was giving him a son. It is still unclear if he was certain Sarah could be the boy's mother. pg 120-126

4. What was Abraham's "vision" problem?

It had been years since he and Sarah were hoping for a child. Abraham had trouble seeing the two of them having a baby. pg 122-125

5. Describe how his uncertainty fed his fear.

All Abraham could see was that he had no child. He had married a barren woman. Childlessness greeted him every morning and reminded him every night that his life was passing, his dream dying. It was a situation and a circumstance he could see. It was a repetitive threat of defeat. He saw it and feared. pg 122

6. Define blind faith.
Blind faith means you believe something even though you have no proof, or reason to believe something. pg 123

7. Does God require us to have blind faith? Why or why not?
No, God's word is always our confidence and evidence. God has given us many reasons or proofs to believe in Him in His word. Also, Romans 1:19-20 informs us the created world is clear evidence, so clear that man is without an excuse for refusing to believe in God. pg 123

8. In your own words, what is the biblical definition of faith?
Answers will vary, but should include the concepts expressed in Hebrews 11:1 such as faith is a strong trust in God, a strong trust in His character, in what He said, an assurance that is a guarantee that supports the things you are confidently, happily expecting and puts this principle to a proving test resulting in what you are believing for becoming visible. pg 124

Activity: Compare fear and faith. Define both. Using a topical index, Bible dictionary or even Google, find verses that deal with both. Jesus told Jairus to fear not. Did He say this to others? Why? The Bible says in 2Timothy 1:7 that God did not give us a spirit of fear. Where do you think fear comes from and what is its purpose? Did fear help Abraham? Identify any areas in your life where you are exhibiting fear and give those places to God. We are able to bring our thoughts into obedience to Jesus and to cast down our imagination when it wanders into fear. (Read 2Corinthians 10:5) *Answers will vary according to student's knowledge and spiritual maturity, but there should be a marked distinction between fear and faith. For example, while both are activated by belief and a confidence in that belief, fear imagines an unwanted outcome. It can be*

said that fear is faith in what you don't want to happen. This is the reason Jesus warns us not to fear. Fear does not come from God because the Bible tells us God did not give us a spirit of fear. Some debate if fear is indeed a spirit. It can be fed by our senses, our imagination and thoughts.
Jesus said many times not to fear or be afraid. This is not fear in the sense of honoring God with reverence. This is fearing in the context of worry, doubt, terror and being scared. Honoring God helped Abraham. Being afraid of men/man or failure did not.

9. Why is imagination important to faith?
Hope is the picture in your head. We think in pictures. What you are capable of picturing matters when it concerns receiving from God because what you can imagine happening will be possible to you. pg 125

10. What is the archaeological evidence for making a servant an heir?
The Nuzi adoption tablets and the adoption contracts from Tell Harmal in Baghdad have shown that it was a legal alternative throughout the Ancient Near East. pg125-126

11. Read the fourth chapter of Romans. Why did God grant righteousness to Abraham?
Romans 4:3 Abraham believed God, and it was counted unto him for righteousness.

12. Why is this imputation of righteousness significant to us and to the concept of grace through faith in Ephesians 2:8? "For by grace are ye saved through faith; and that not of yourselves: it is the gift of God."
We are made righteous through faith in Jesus and by the grace offered to us.

Activity: Beginning in Genesis 12, read all the conversations between God and Abraham. What conclusions can you make about God?
Answers will vary but should include the idea that God's intent is for our good.

13. Briefly outline what a blood covenant is, its importance, and how it was used in Abraham's day.
Covenant means cutting as in a compact, alliance or treaty made by passing between pieces of flesh. The purpose of the covenant was to bind two parties together for their common good. It was a pledge of protection, loyalty, provision and friendship. Since life is found in the blood, the fellowship agreement was for life. If a man broke it, he was killed. In Genesis 15:9-18 God directs Abraham to sacrifice a heifer, a goat, a ram, a dove and a pigeon, but not as a burnt sacrifice. Abraham killed them, cut them (except the birds) and arranged them. After dark, a supernatural smoking furnace and a torch passed between the pieces. pg 128-130

14. What details did God give Abraham during their encounter in Genesis 15?
God gave Abraham specific territorial boundaries concerning the land he was to inherit, a vision of his descendents' future, and assurance that he, out of his own body would have a son. pg 126,130

15. What seems to have happened in Sarah's life during this time and what did she do to "solve" it?
She seems to have experienced menopause. She gave her servant Hagar to Abraham in order to have a child. pg131

16. Is there archaeological evidence of such a custom as Sarah chose?

Yes, an Assyrian cuneiform tablet of a marriage contract was discovered that described a similar arrangement as Sarah made with Hagar. pg132

17. Describe Hagar and her reaction to her promotion in Abraham's household.
When she found out she was pregnant, she mocked Sarah. pg132

18. What was Sarah's response to Hagar's abuse? Do you think Sarah was harsh? Why or why not?
The Bible says Sarah was hard on her. Answers will vary. pg132-134

19. How do we know Abraham and Sarah did not make the right choices concerning Hagar?
God wanted Sarah and Abraham to be the parents of the son He had chosen to inherit His promises. This son's name would be Isaac. pg136-138

20. Why was Abraham's obedience critical when he was ninety-nine?
He needed to chose the authority speaking into his life, the one to whom he would be obedient. He had listened to Sarah, his own desire to have a son and the cultural practices around him concerning Hagar. He had not obeyed God. God required obedience to inherit the promises. 136-137

21. Why did God change their names?
Their new names were a more accurate picture of God's purpose for them. He changed their names to change their perspective and to speak His desire over them as their authority figure. 137-138

22. What did God tell Abraham to do as a sign of his part of the covenant? State the archaeological evidence of this practice.

He wanted Abraham to circumcise himself and every male born or bought in his household. This was to be God's covenant with Abraham and his offspring. His children would carry a mark on their body as a sign of their continuing covenant with God. Images depicting circumcision were discovered on walls in Egypt dating to Djedkare of the Fifth Dynasty, and on a scene on an Egyptian palette of naked Semitic captives dated to the era just before the First Dynasties in Egypt. In the Amuq valley, bronze statues dating to 3200 BC were discovered showing circumcised men with beards. pg 138-139

23. What made Abraham laugh when God was talking to him?
That he and Sarah would have a baby together. pg142-143

24. How do we know Abraham either did not understand or did not accept what God was telling him about Sarah?
He asked God to bless Ishmael. pg 142-143

25. Describe the Lord's visit to Abraham and Sarah in Genesis 18.
Answer should include following points: The Lord appeared with two other men who were angels. Abraham and Sarah prepared food for them and as they ate, the Lord asked about Sarah. He told Abraham and Sarah that Sarah would have a baby during that time the following year. Sarah laughed and the Lord asked why. She denied laughing, but the Lord encouraged her by reminding her nothing is impossible for God. Later He told Abraham He was going to Sodom and destroy it. Abraham, knowing it was a sinful place, asked God not to destroy it if there were ten righteous people living there. pg143-145

Chapter 6 Test Questions

1. What bothered Abraham after he returned from rescuing Lot?
He wanted God to give him a son.

2. What was Abraham's "vision" problem?
It had been years since he and Sarah were hoping for a child. Abraham had trouble seeing the two of them having a baby.

3. In your own words, what is the biblical definition of faith?
Answers will vary, but should include the concepts expressed in Hebrews 11:1 such as faith is a strong trust in God, a strong trust in His character, in what He said, an assurance that is a guarantee that supports the things you are confidently, happily expecting and puts this principle to a proving test resulting in what you are believing for becoming visible.

4. Why is imagination important to faith?
Hope is the picture in your head. We think in pictures. What you are capable of picturing matters when it concerns receiving from God because what you can imagine happening will be possible to you.

5. What is the archaeological evidence for making a servant an heir?
The Nuzi adoption tablets and the adoption contracts from Tell Harmal in Baghdad have shown that it was a legal alternative throughout the Ancient Near East.

6. What details did God give Abraham during their encounter in Genesis 15?
God gave Abraham specific territorial boundaries concerning the land he was to inherit, a vision of his descendents' future, and assurance that he, out

of his own body would have a son.

7. What seems to have happened in Sarah's life during this time and what did she do to "solve" it?
She seems to have experienced menopause. She gave her servant Hagar to Abraham in order to have a child.

8. Is there archaeological evidence of such a custom as Sarah chose?
Yes, an Assyrian cuneiform tablet of a marriage contract was discovered that described a similar arrangement as Sarah made with Hagar.

9. What did God tell Abraham to do as a sign of his part of the covenant? State the archaeological evidence of this practice.
He wanted Abraham to circumcise himself and every male born or bought in his household. This was to be God's covenant with Abraham and his offspring. His children would carry a mark on their body as a sign of their continuing covenant with God. Images depicting circumcision were discovered on walls in Egypt dating to Djedkare of the Fifth Dynasty, and on a scene on an Egyptian palette of naked Semitic captives dated to the era just before the First Dynasties in Egypt. In the Amuq valley, bronze statues dating to 3200 BC were discovered showing circumcised men with beards.

10. Why was Abraham's obedience critical when he was ninety-nine?
He needed to chose the authority speaking into his life, the one to whom he would be obedient. He had listened to Sarah, his own desire to have a son and the cultural practices around him concerning Hagar. He had not obeyed God. God required obedience to inherit the promises.

Optional essay question: How do we know Abraham and Sarah did not make the right choices concerning Hagar? Or, In your own words, what is the biblical definition of faith?

How do we know Abraham and Sarah did not make the right choices concerning Hagar?
Answers should include: God wanted Sarah and Abraham to be the parents of the son He had chosen to inherit His promises. This son's name would be Isaac.

Or, In your own words, what is the biblical definition of faith?
Answers will vary, but should include the concepts expressed in Hebrews 11:1 such as faith is a strong trust in God, a strong trust in His character, in what He said, an assurance that is a guarantee that supports the things you are confidently, happily expecting and puts this principle to a proving test resulting in what you are believing for becoming visible.

Chapter 7 General Questions

1. Skeptics of the Bible think the account of Lot in the Bible was copied from Ovid's poem. Ovid was a Greek writer born about 43BC. Why is the skeptics' theory impossible even by their own dating method?
Ovid was born about 43 BC. The Dead Sea Scrolls prove Lot's story was written much earlier around 600 BC. Ovid lived after Lot and too late for Lot's story to have copied Ovid's. pg 149

2. Why was the Lord on His way to Sodom?
He had heard some bad reports and was going to check it out. If it was as bad as the angels had reported when they came before Him, He was going to have it destroyed. pg 150

3. What was Sodom famous for?
Sin. pg 151

4. One of Sodom's sins was an abundance of idleness. The Hebrew word translated idleness is *shâqat*. What does it mean?
This is an idleness that appeases, is not disturbed and remains quiet. pg 151

5. God promised Abraham He would spare the city if how many people were found to be righteous?
Ten. pg 151

6. Where does the Bible say the five cities on the plain are located?
East of the Dead Sea. pg 152

7. List the faults of Dr. Steven Collins' theory concerning the location for Sodom.
- *It is north of the location for Sodom listed in other verses of the Bible such as Genesis 14.*
- *The supposed discoveries are in the wrong time period.*
- *The geography is not as compelling as Dr. Collins proposes because it directly contradicts historical and archaeological references to the cities. pg153*

8. Why is Zoar important in the search for Sodom and what does archaeology and ancient literature have to say about the city?
Zoar was inhabited until the Middle Ages. Numerous extra-biblical sources mention Zoar and its location south of the Dead Sea and east of the Jordan. Josephus described a lake he called Asphaltitis which is the Dead Sea and said it stretched as far as Zoar in Arabia. He said Sodom was in the area but had been destroyed. Zoar was located in the Roman province of Palaestina Salutaris in an area covering south of the Dead Sea, the Negev and Petra. Eusebius translated the Hebrew Tsô'ar (Zoar) into Greek as Zogera, Zogora, Segor and Sigor and said it was one of the five cities of the plain, referring to Genesis 14. He also put it south of the Dead Sea. Four hundred years after Eusebius, Egeria wrote to her girlfriends about the bishop of Zoara. At the time of the Crusades, Zoar was called Palmer and recognized for its delicious dates by famous archbishops like William of Tyre and Arabic mapmakers. Zoar is on the oldest map of the Holy Land at St. George's church in Madaba, Jordan. pg 153-155

9. How do the Ebla Tablets help scholars locate the five cities?
Among Ebla Tablets is a tablet listing trade cities and routes. It describes one route south through the central hill country of modern day Israel, along

the west shore of the Dead Sea and then circling its southern edge to travel north along the eastern shore. Two cities are named on the eastern side: Admah and Sodom. *pg 155*

10. What two modern places are thought to be the ancient ruins of Sodom and Gomorrah?
Many archaeologists and scholars have concluded Bâb edh-Dhrâ' is ancient Sodom and Numeira is Gomorrah. pg 156, 159

11. Describe the archaeological discoveries at Sodom and Gomorrah.
There were cities, cultured urban centers, homes where people grew grains, orchards of olives, grapes, peaches and figs. There were signs that some residents were semi-nomadic shepherds. A thick wall surrounded Bâb edh-Dhrâ' and about a thousand people lived there. More lived outside the city. Each of the five cities were located by rivers and the land was completely irrigated. The excavations at Bâb edh-Dhrâ' showed walls and towers collapsed violently; fire began on roofs, and as the roofs caved in, fire burned the interior of the buildings. Ash still covers the area. It was in every building uncovered. pg 156-158

12. What do geologists and archaeologist Bryant Wood believe to be the immediate cause of the destruction of the cities?
An earthquake might have destroyed the cities, and sulfurous oil exploded from underground and rained on four of the cities. pg157-159

13. Do you think there is enough evidence to come to this conclusion?
Answers may vary.

14. Was there evidence at Sodom and Gomorrah of an earlier attack like the one Chedorlaomer carried out against these cities?
Dr. Wood believes there was evidence at both sites for a previous destruction, appearing similar to the description of Chedorlaomer's attack twenty years before. Signs of fire damage on stones and rebuilt walls were found amid the final destruction. pg 159

15. What is the evidence that Philistines were in Canaan during Abraham's lifetime?
The Philistines are related to the Egyptians. Archaeology has uncovered pottery connected to the Egyptian culture in large settlements in the northern Sinai region where the Bible says the Philistines came from. Archaeologists have also noted the same settlements in southern Canaan near the time of the Jemdat Nasr period and First Dynasty of Egypt, and other extrabiblical sources put the Philistines in Canaan. pg 163

16. What is the difference between Philistines and Phoenicians?
The Phoenicians were Canaanites living in Lebanon and the Philistines were not Canaanites but they moved there. pg 162-163

17. Describe the volatile situation with Ishmael and Hagar.
Hagar mocked Sarah and her position. As Abraham's concubine and the mother of Ishmael, she may have been eagerly waiting for the death of either Abraham or Sarah. After Isaac was born, Ishmael was no longer the heir to Abraham's fortune. He did not treat Isaac well. pg 165-167

18. How do we know from the Bible that Ishmael's actions toward Isaac were not innocent?
Galatians 4:29 says Ishmael persecuted Isaac. "But as then he that was

born after the flesh persecuted him that was born after the Spirit..." The word used in Genesis (tsachaq) shows it was not harmless jesting. It may even have involved physical contact. pg 167

19. What does "breaking the clump" mean?
Breaking the clump was the term used to sever family ties with the intent of disinheriting an heir. pg 167

20. How did the consequences of Abraham's choices affect him, Sarah, Isaac, Hagar and Ishmael?
Sarah and Isaac were mistreated. Abraham divorced Hagar and sent her and Ishmael away into the wilderness. They all suffered emotionally. pg 166-168

21. Do you think Sarah's response to the situation was justified? Why or why not?
Answers may vary.

22. How was God kind to Ishmael? To Hagar?
Answers may vary but should include mercy and blessing.

Activity: How might you have tried to solve this family squabble? Try to think how your solution would have played out five years later. Do you think any scenario other than full control would have satisfied Ishmael and Hagar? Why or why not? *Answers will vary.*

23. What does *châmâs* mean?
Cruel unrighteous, injustice, violence. pg 133, 167

Activity: Research and read news articles and headlines happening in Israel and the Middle East today. Do you see any examples of *châmâs* today? Make a list of things to pray for to help the people of the Middle East settle their differences. *Answers will vary.*

24. Why do we say Ishmael was "born of the flesh?"
He was the son born from man's decision, not God's. pg 167

25. What comparisons can you draw between Ishmael and Hagar and blended families, step families or families that separate and remarry? What would you say to Ishmael to help him and to encourage or comfort him? *Answers will vary.*

Chapter 7 Test Questions

1. Why was the Lord on His way to Sodom?
He had heard some bad reports and was going to check it out. If it was as bad as the angels had reported when they came before Him, He was going to have it destroyed.

2. How do we know from the Bible that Ishmael's actions toward Isaac were not innocent?
Galatians 4:29 says Ishmael persecuted Isaac. "But as then he that was born after the flesh persecuted him that was born after the Spirit..." The word used in Genesis (tsachaq) shows it was not harmless jesting. It may even have involved physical contact.

3. What is the evidence that Philistines were in Canaan during Abraham's lifetime?
The Philistines are related to the Egyptians. Archaeology has uncovered pottery connected to the Egyptian culture in large settlements in the northern Sinai region where the Bible says the Philistines came from. Archaeologists have also noted the same settlements in southern Canaan near the time of the Jemdat Nasr period and First Dynasty of Egypt, and other extra-biblical sources put the Philistines in Canaan.

4. How did the consequences of Abraham's choices affect him, Sarah, Isaac, Hagar and Ishmael?
Sarah and Isaac were mistreated. Abraham divorced Hagar and sent her and Ishmael away into the wilderness. They all suffered emotionally.

5. Why do we say Ishmael was "born of the flesh?"
He was the son born from man's decision, not God's.

6. Where does the Bible say the five cities on the plain are located?
East of the Dead Sea.

7. The Hebrew word translated idleness is *shâqat*. What does it mean?
This is an idleness that appeases, is not disturbed and remains quiet.

8. How do the Ebla Tablets help scholars locate the five cities?
Among Ebla Tablets is a tablet listing trade cities and routes. It describes one route south through the central hill country of modern day Israel, along the west shore of the Dead Sea and then circling its southern edge to travel north along the eastern shore. Two cities are named on the eastern side: Admah and Sodom.

9. What two modern places are thought to be the ancient ruins of Sodom and Gomorrah?
Many archaeologists and scholars have concluded Bâb edh-Dhrâ' is ancient Sodom and Numeira is Gomorrah.

10. Was there evidence at Sodom and Gomorrah of an earlier attack like the one Chedorlaomer carried out against these cities? Explain your answer.
Dr. Wood believes there was evidence at both sites for a previous destruction, appearing similar to the description of Chedorlaomer's attack twenty years before. Signs of fire damage on stones and rebuilt walls were found amid the final destruction.

Optional essay question: Why is Zoar important in the search for Sodom and what does archaeology and ancient literature have to say about the city?

Zoar was inhabited until the Middle Ages. Numerous extra-biblical sources mention Zoar and its location south of the Dead Sea and east of the Jordan. Josephus described a lake he called Asphaltitis which is the Dead Sea and said it stretched as far as Zoar in Arabia. He said Sodom was in the area but had been destroyed. Zoar was located in the Roman province of Palaestina Salutaris in an area covering south of the Dead Sea, the Negev and Petra. Eusebius translated the Hebrew Tsô'ar (Zoar) into Greek as Zogera, Zogora, Segor and Sigor and said it was one of the five cities of the plain, referring to Genesis 14. He also put it south of the Dead Sea. Four hundred years after Eusebius, Egeria wrote to her girlfriends about the bishop of Zoara. At the time of the Crusades, Zoar was called Palmer and recognized for its delicious dates by famous archbishops like William of Tyre and Arabic mapmakers. Zoar is on the oldest map of the Holy Land at St. George's church in Madaba, Jordan.

Chapter 8 General Questions

1. Why is Mt. Moriah an important place?
It is the location of the Foundation Stone which Jews believe to be the site of the Holy of Holies of the First Temple. They also believe it is where God created Adam. It was where Melchizedek ruled as King of Salem and High Priest of the Most High God. Archaeology has proven Mt. Moriah, the site of the Temple Mount, to be the location of the First and Second Temples. For Christians it is where Jesus was dedicated as a baby and where He sat with the priests when he was twelve years old. Jesus prayed and taught on Mt. Moriah many times, and it was the place where Jewish Christians began to meet after Jesus' resurrection. pg 171-172

2. Explain Islam's story about Muhammad visiting the Temple Mount and why it couldn't have happened.
Muslims believe Muhammad visited the Jewish temple and met Abraham. But neither temple existed at the time of Muhammad. Later, the location was changed to the Al-Aqsa Mosque, but it wasn't built yet. pg 172-173

3. According to archaeology, what is the oldest mention of Jerusalem outside of the Bible?
A papyrus fragment of a shipping receipt dating to the seventh century BC. The fragment was a government correspondence between the king's maidservant for an order of wine from Na'arat to Jerusalem, the capital of Judah. pg 173-174

4. What is the "Binding of Isaac?"
The account of Abraham's offering of Isaac as a sacrifice in obedience to God. Also called The Akedah. pg 174-175

5. Why did God call Isaac Abraham's only son?
He was the only son of the promise with a miraculous birth. pg 175

6. Do you think Abraham understood the concept of what we call the Triune God– Father, Son and Holy Spirit? Why or why not?
The idea of a triune God, Father, Son and Holy Spirit was not known to believers of Old Testament days. It was hidden in scripture, but not understood until Jesus came and introduced people to the Father and the Spirit, calling Himself the Son. Because it was not part of their traditional theology, the Pharisees in Jesus' day rejected the concept, looking instead for an earthly Messiah. pg 175

7. How is testing in the Old Testament related to obedience?
Nacah in English can mean test, assay, prove, try and adventure. We prove our obedience to God's word, what He tells us to do in a given situation or according to His standards. This is the pattern of "testing" from God. We either obey Him or we don't. The consequences are up to us. Example: Exodus 15:25-26 "And he cried unto the LORD; and the LORD shewed him a tree, which when he had cast into the waters, the waters were made sweet: there he made for them a statute and an ordinance, and there he proved them, And said, If thou wilt diligently hearken to the voice of the LORD thy God, and wilt do that which is right in his sight, and wilt give ear to his commandments, and keep all his statutes, I will put none of these diseases upon thee, which I have brought upon the Egyptians: for I am the LORD that healeth thee." pg 176

8. What is the difference between testing and temptation?
Temptation arises from evil desires within us while a test comes from pressure applied through outside circumstances. pg 176

9. How old was Isaac when Abraham made the trip to Mt. Moriah?
All we truly know is old enough to carry wood. Scholars and rabbis debate ages from adolescence to mid to late thirties. pg 177

Activity: Name the similarities between the Binding of Isaac and the events of Jesus' crucifixion. *pg 177*

- *It was a three day journey from Beersheba to Moriah and both Isaac and Jesus were alive after three days.*
- *Abraham was pondering death and loss for three days like Jesus' followers,*
- *Isaac carried wood on his shoulder up a mountain like Jesus carried His cross to Golgotha.*
- *Moriah is in Jerusalem.*
- *Abraham walked with Isaac as God the Father was with Jesus.*
- *In both instances it was the loving father offering their miraculous, only sons of promise.*
- *Abraham carried fire, a symbol of the Holy Spirit.*
- *Abraham believed Isaac would be raised from the dead.*

10. How do we know Abraham believed God would raise Isaac from the dead?
He said, "I and the lad will go yonder and worship, and come again to you." (Genesis 22:5) Hebrews 11:17-19 says "By faith Abraham, when he was tried, offered up Isaac: and he that had received the promises offered up his only begotten son, Of whom it was said, That in Isaac shall thy seed be called: Accounting that God was able to raise him up, even from the dead; from whence also he received him in a figure." pg 178

11. What do you think gave Abraham the courage to be obedient to God's command to offer Isaac?
Answers may vary, but should include the concept of what God had already done for Abraham.

12. How do we know Isaac was willing to do what his father asked?
He was bound and laid on the altar. pg 178

13. When did Jesus' followers begin to understand the meaning of the Binding of Isaac?
After Jesus was raised from the dead. pg 180

14. What is the significance of God providing the male sheep on Mt. Moriah?
The male sheep in the thicket was God's provision, the Lamb He intended to provide. pg181

15. Is the sculpture called Ram in a Thicket that was found by Leonard C. Woolley proof Abraham's story is made up? Explain your answer.
No. Woolley gave it that name. Scholars believe the goat depicted in the statue is not caught but eating the leaves of the thicket, a common sight in the area even in modern times. It proves the possibility of a ram becoming caught in the branches of a thicket by his horns as he browsed for his meal. pg 181

16. How does the Hebrew word 'ayil give testimony to Jesus?
Its root word is el which is God or god. According to the Ancient Hebrew Lexicon of the Bible by Jeff A. Benner, it means strong one. The Biblical Hebrew E-Magazine defines it literally as "one that stands tall in might."

Answer Keys

The ram was a picture of Jesus. pg182

17. What is the connection between Rosh Hashanah and the Binding of Isaac?
The Binding of Isaac is retold during the second day of Rosh Hashanah. The ram's horn, a symbol of the one caught in the thicket, is blown as a reminder of how Isaac was spared. pg 182

18. What name did Abraham give Mt. Moriah and what did it mean?
Abraham named the place Jehovahjireh which translators have defined in English as the Lord will provide. pg 182

19. Why do you think the Bible's statement that Abraham mourned "Sarah" is significant?
Answers may vary. pg 184

20. Describe the Cave of the Patriarchs.
It is the only land and cave Abraham bought in Canaan. He bought it so he could bury Sarah. Abraham and Sarah were buried at Machpelah as well as Isaac and Rebekah and Jacob and Leah. Jews have always honored the site. Herod built a tomb over it which still stands today, 2,000 years after it was built. But by 1260 Muslim Mamelukes took over, and Jews and Christians were banned from visiting the tomb. It is also called Machpelah which means doubled. There are two caves. The Israel Antiquities Authority dated the burial site to the Early Bronze Age. pg 186-187

21. What is the longest part of Abraham's story in Genesis?
The longest narrative in Abraham's story is about this servant's trip back to Aram-Naharaim. pg188

22. Is their archaeological evidence for a servant choosing a wife? If so, explain how it applies to Abraham.
Sending a servant to pick a wife was not that unusual. There is evidence of kings using servants to arrange marriages in the Amarna Letters. In EA 31, for example, is the negotiation of marriage between an Egyptian king and a Hittite king through a messenger named IrSappa. Professor Jack Sasson wrote about kings at Mari using messengers. Abraham acted like a king when he rescued Lot and here we see him doing it again. pg188

23. Who was Rebekah?
Abraham's brother Nahor's granddaughter. She became Isaac's wife. pg 189

24. Who was Keturah?
Abraham's secondary wife and concubine. pg 190

25. Briefly outline Isaac's life compared to Abraham's.
Answers may vary. Isaac became afraid for his life in Gerar too. He also had a beautiful, rich wife. He decided to lie, and use Abraham's ruse, declaring Rebekah was his sister. Isaac and his wife also had problems having children at first. But Isaac's life was rather dull compared to his father's. He never battled kings. He never left Canaan. He never changed his name; perhaps because God named him. He never had concubines. His twelve grandsons would become the twelve tribes of Israel. His life was mostly peaceful, until his sons grew up and started fighting over their rights. Isaac was the longest lived patriarch. pg 189-190

Activity: List Abraham's sons and their lands. What details do we know about them?

He sent them to the lands east of Canaan. Ishmael had twelve sons who became a great nation. When Abraham died, Ishmael was there with Isaac to bury him in the Cave of Machpelah. he had six more sons. These sons became nations in Arabia. Near the end of his life, the Bible says he gave gifts to them and Ishmael. "But unto the sons of the concubines, which Abraham had, Abraham gave gifts, and sent them away from Isaac his son, while he yet lived, eastward, unto the east country." (Genesis 25:6) One of Abraham's sons by Keturah was Midian, the father of the Midianites. Midian was located in modern day northwest Saudi Arabia. Abraham's grandsons, Sheba and Dedan, are also associated with territories inside Saudi Arabia. pg 169, 190

Drawing Near Activity: What difficult thing have you been asked to do? How did you handle it?
Many times people say they want to know God's will for their lives. They may not realize knowing His will opens them to the responsibility of willfully obeying or disobeying it. Never seeking God's will for your life is one kind of wrong, but knowing and disobeying is another. Ask Jonah. Read the book of Jonah in the Old Testament if you haven't heard his story. What happened to Jonah and why?
The truth is, you will never be truly happy or fulfilled until you accept God's purpose for your life: to accept His love for you. God never intended that you do the difficult things on your own. He wants to travel with you to your Mt. Moriah because He has already provided everything you need to leave there in victory. *Answers will vary. Jonah heard what God told him to do and decided not to do it. He went his own way without God's blessing and ended up in the belly of a whale. When he repented, God delivered him. Then Jonah delivered the message to Ninevah that God had given him.*

Chapter 8 Test Questions

1. Why is Mt. Moriah an important place?
It is the location of the Foundation Stone which Jews believe to be the site of the Holy of Holies of the First Temple. They also believe it is where God created Adam. It was where Melchizedek ruled as King of Salem and High Priest of the Most High God. Archaeology has proven Mt. Moriah, the site of the Temple Mount, to be the location of the First and Second Temples. For Christians it is where Jesus was dedicated as a baby and where He sat with the priests when he was twelve years old. Jesus prayed and taught on Mt. Moriah many times, and it was the place where Jewish Christians began to meet after Jesus' resurrection. pg 171-172

2. What name did Abraham give Mt. Moriah and what did it mean?
Abraham named the place Jehovahjireh which translators have defined in English as the Lord will provide. pg 182

3. What is the "Binding of Isaac?"
The account of Abraham's offering of Isaac as a sacrifice in obedience to God. Also called The Akedah. pg 174-175

4. Why did God call Isaac Abraham's only son?
He was the only son of the promise with a miraculous birth. pg 175

5. What is the difference between testing and temptation?
Temptation arises from evil desires within us while a test comes from pressure applied through outside circumstances. pg 176

6. How do we know Abraham believed God would raise Isaac from the dead?

He was bound and laid on the altar. pg 178

7. Who was Keturah?
Abraham's secondary wife and concubine. pg 190

8. What is the connection between Rosh Hashanah and the Binding of Isaac?
The Binding of Isaac is retold during the second day of Rosh Hashanah. The ram's horn, a symbol of the one caught in the thicket, is blown as a reminder of how Isaac was spared. pg 182

9. When did Jesus' followers begin to understand the meaning of the Binding of Isaac?
After Jesus was raised from the dead. pg 180

10. How does the Hebrew word 'ayil give testimony to Jesus?
Its root word is el which is God or god. According to the Ancient Hebrew Lexicon of the Bible by Jeff A. Benner, it means strong one. The Biblical Hebrew E-Magazine defines it literally as "one that stands tall in might." The ram was a picture of Jesus. pg182

Optional essay question: Briefly outline Isaac's life compared to Abraham's. Or, Why do you think the Bible's statement that Abraham mourned "Sarah" is significant?

Briefly outline Isaac's life compared to Abraham's.
Answers may vary. Isaac became afraid for his life in Gerar too. He also had a beautiful, rich wife. He decided to lie, and use Abraham's ruse, declaring Rebekah was his sister. Isaac and his wife also had problems having

children at first. But Isaac's life was rather dull compared to his father's. He never battled kings. He never left Canaan. He never changed his name; perhaps because God named him. He never had concubines. His twelve grandsons would become the twelve tribes of Israel. His life was mostly peaceful, until his sons grew up and started fighting over their rights. Isaac was the longest lived patriarch.

Or, Why do you think the Bible's statement that Abraham mourned "Sarah" is significant?
Answers may vary. pg 184

Chapter 9 General Questions

1. Read Galatians 3. In your own words, explain the concept of being Abraham's seed and heirs according to the promise.
Answers may vary but should include something similar to "If we are born again, we are heirs to Abraham's promise of all God's desires toward him through faith by grace."

2. What title do Christians give Abraham?
The father of all who have faith. pg195

3. Why is Abraham important to the people living in the Middle East?
Many share him as their flesh and blood ancestor. pg 196-197 and pg 66-67

4. What are some misconceptions about Abraham?
He is the father of three religions; Muslims say he built the Kaaba; Jews add to his story; Christian theologians have used his account to serve a social gospel and liberal theology. pg 196-199

5. What significant biblical character was still living when Abraham lived?
The Bible tells us Abraham's life overlapped with Shem's. pg 199

6. Discoveries at what archaeological sites have supported the Bible's account of Abraham and given us more insight?
The setting and cultural practices revealed in Abraham's account are supported by ancient texts and discoveries at Ebla, Mari, Nuzi, Ugarit, Ur

and other sites in northern Mesopotamia. pg 200

7. If the details of Abraham's story have been backed up by archaeology, what does that suggest about the rest of his account?
It is all true and worth investigating. pg 200

8. Briefly explain what archaeology has added to our knowledge of Abraham.
Abraham dates to the Early Bronze Age 1 and the Early Dynasty period in Egypt. Cities were thriving and civilizations were spreading farther and farther. Trade routes were well established; schools taught foreign languages and advanced math. The setting and cultural practices revealed in Abraham's account are supported by ancient texts and discoveries at Ebla, Mari, Nuzi, Ugarit, Ur and other sites in northern Mesopotamia. pg 199-200

9. What was Abraham's path to success?
His path to success came when God spoke to him, he understood what to do and he believed God would do what He said in every area of his life. Then he acted on it. pg 201

10. What did Abraham have to receive?
Abraham had to receive what God had already done for him. pg 202

11. List what Abraham has taught us about faith and briefly describe each in your own words.
Answers will vary but should be based on the following main points:
- *Total obedience is crucial.*
- *Abraham teaches us is to ask questions.*

- *Abraham had to receive what God had already done for him.*
- *Abraham had to learn a higher law controlled and commanded the physical world.*
- *Abraham had to choose the authority speaking into his life.*
- *Abraham had to continue to stick with God. pg 201-206*

Activity: Read Romans 4:18-22. Of this New Testament account of Abraham, what stands out to you right now? Make it a point of prayer to God.
Answers will vary.

12. What has Abraham taught us about covenants?
A covenant is an agreement between two parties. They are forever binding. People involved in the covenant become one blood and therefore family who were assured protection and provision. pg 206

13. What do you think is the most important part of Abraham's legacy?
Answers will vary.

14. List seven things Abraham teaches us about faith.
1. *God requires complete and total trust.*
2. *Total obedience is crucial.*
3. *Abraham teaches us is to ask questions.*
4. *Abraham had to receive what God had already done for him.*
5. *Abraham had to learn a higher law controlled and commanded the physical world.*
6. *Abraham had to choose the authority speaking into his life.*
7. *Abraham had to continue to stick with God. pg 201-206*

Chapter 9 Test Questions

1. What does this verse mean "If we are Christ's then we are Abraham's seed and heirs according to the promise?" (Galatians 3:29)
If we are born again, we are heirs to Abraham's promise of all God's desires toward him through faith by grace.

2. List seven things Abraham teaches us about faith.
1. God requires complete and total trust.
2. Total obedience is crucial.
3. Abraham teaches us is to ask questions.
4. Abraham had to receive what God had already done for him.
5. Abraham had to learn a higher law controlled and commanded the physical world.
6. Abraham had to choose the authority speaking into his life.
7. Abraham had to continue to stick with God.

3. Discoveries at what archaeological sites have supported the Bible's account of Abraham and given us more insight?
The setting and cultural practices revealed in Abraham's account are supported by ancient texts and discoveries at Ebla, Mari, Nuzi, Ugarit, Ur and other sites in northern Mesopotamia.

4. Why is Abraham important to the people living in the Middle East?
Many share him as their flesh and blood ancestor.

5. What are some misconceptions about Abraham?
He is the father of three religions; Muslims say he built the Kaaba; Jews add

to his story; Christian theologians have used his account to serve a social gospel and liberal theology.

6. What significant biblical character was still living when Abraham lived?
The Bible tells us Abraham's life overlapped with Shem's.

7. Outline Abraham's path to success.
His path to success came when God spoke to him, he understood what to do and he believed God would do what He said in every area of his life. Then he acted on it.

8. If the details of Abraham's story have been backed up by archaeology, what does that suggest about the rest of his account?
It is all true and worth investigating.

9. What title do Christians give Abraham?
The father of all who have faith.

10. What was vital that Abraham receive from God?
Abraham had to receive what God had already done for him.

Optional essay question: What do you think is the most important part of Abraham's legacy? Or, What is a covenant and what has Abraham taught us about them?

What do you think is the most important part of Abraham's legacy?
Answers will vary.

Or, What is a covenant and what has Abraham taught us about them? *A covenant is an agreement between two parties. They are forever binding. People involved in the covenant become one blood and therefore family who were assured protection and provision.*

Thank you for purchasing *From Abram to Abraham Study Guide*.

If you found it helpful, please leave a review online where you found the book. For more titles visit our website at https://www.flyingeagle-publications.com. You can check out our blog or join our community. We would love to hear from you.

www.ingramcontent.com/pod-product-compliance
Lightning Source LLC
Chambersburg PA
CBHW071240070526
4483CB00017B/2268